The Machine Shed Roots

We opened the Iowa Machine Shed Restaurant in 1978 in rural Davenport, Iowa with just over 100 seats. Our location wasn't great and much of the equipment was old (but clean) and broke too often.

We were all pretty young and green. But we started with a powerful commitment; that commitment was a simple five word constitution- "Dedicated to the Iowa Farmer." That dedication meant that we worked to have a restaurant that wasn't just "farm" themed but would be something that farmers could be proud of. That meant using only the best pork and beef, real whipped cream on the pies, hearty soups, fresh baked goods made from scratch, and little things like genuine mashed potatoes and real butter. Although we still had a lot to learn, that dedication guided us through the early days. Even though money was tight, we were never tempted to take a cheaper route.

Thanks to you, folks like The Machine Shed from the start. The original Machine shed has been expanded and improved many times. And now, other Machine Sheds have sprung up in Des Moines, Iowa; Olathe, Kansas; Rockford Illinois; Pewaukee and Appleton, Wisconsin. Along the way we have been delighted to have received a bushel basketful of honors from farm groups like the Pork Producers and the Beef Industry Council. We're constantly trying to live up to those honors on the food we prepare and in the way we prepare and the way we bring it to you.

Mike Whalen

Thanks for your help

Heart of America

Restaurants & Inns™
True midwestern hospitality

Visit all of Heart of America's properties throughout the midwest

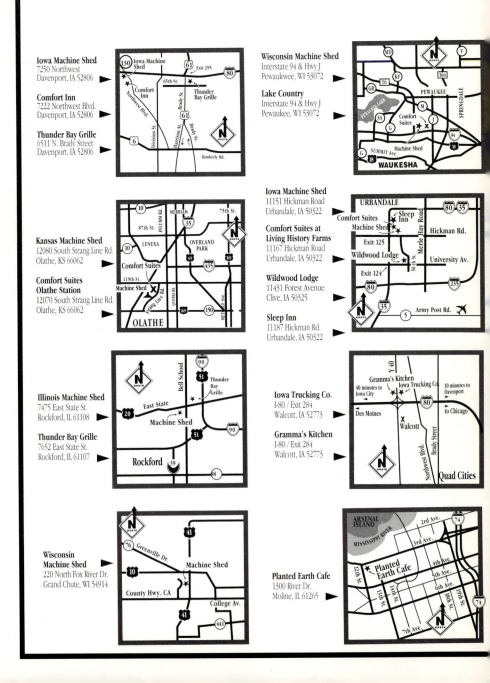

Iowa Machine Shed
7250 Northwest
Davenport, IA 52806

Comfort Inn
7222 Northwest Blvd.
Davenport, IA 52806

Thunder Bay Grille
6511 N. Brady Street
Davenport, IA 52806

Wisconsin Machine Shed
Interstate 94 & Hwy J
Pewaukwee, WI 53072

Lake Country
Interstate 94 & Hwy J
Pewaukee, WI 53072

Kansas Machine Shed
12080 South Strang Line Rd.
Olathe, KS 66062

Comfort Suites Olathe Station
12070 South Strang Line Rd.
Olathe, KS 66062

Iowa Machine Shed
11151 Hickman Road
Urbandale, IA 50322

Comfort Suites at Living History Farms
11167 Hickman Road
Urbandale, IA 50322

Wildwood Lodge
11431 Forest Avenue
Clive, IA 50325

Sleep Inn
11187 Hickman Rd.
Urbandale, IA 50322

Illinois Machine Shed
7475 East State St.
Rockford, IL 61108

Thunder Bay Grille
7652 East State St.
Rockford, IL 61107

Iowa Trucking Co.
I-80 / Exit 284
Walcott, IA 52773

Gramma's Kitchen
I-80 / Exit 284
Walcott, IA 52773

Wisconsin Machine Shed
220 North Fox River Dr.
Grand Chute, WI 54914

Planted Earth Cafe
1300 River Dr.
Moline, IL 61265

There is nothing quite as warming to the soul as recalling country holidays with family and friends. Our favorite farm wife and food enthusiast, **Mary Schneckloth**, has conjured up some delightfully nostalgic holiday memories to share with you. In *Country Holiday Favorites*, Mary brings to your table year round food treasures sure to bring your friends and family back year after year.

Notes &
Recipes

_____

_____

_____

_____

_____

_____

_____

_____

_____

_____

_____

_____

_____

_____

_____

_____

_____

_____

_____

Table of Contents

List Your Favorite Recipes

Recipes   **Page**

_____   _____

_____   _____

_____   _____

_____   _____

_____   _____

_____   _____

_____   _____

_____   _____

_____   _____

_____   _____

_____   _____

_____   _____

_____   _____

_____   _____

_____   _____

_____   _____

_____   _____

APPETIZERS

List Your Favorite Recipes

Recipes   **Page**

Apple Dip

8 oz. cream cheese
3/4 c. dark brown sugar
1 tsp. vanilla

1/2 c. crushed peanuts (you may place in food processor for this)

MIX together well and serve with 5 to 6 mixed red and green apples, with skins left on, sliced and dipped in orange or lemon juice to keep them from getting brown.

Artichoke Cheese Dip

1 (8 oz.) can plain artichoke hearts, drained & cut (use scissors)
1 (8 oz.) pkg. shredded Mozzarella cheese
1/8 tsp. onion powder

1/4 c. shredded Cheddar cheese
1/4 c. Parmesan cheese
1/2 c. mayonnaise
Garlic powder, to taste
1/8 tsp. curry powder (opt.)

MIX all ingredients together and put in a casserole dish, I like to cover with cheese.
BAKE at 350° for 30 minutes, until hot and bubbly.
SERVE with corn chips or your favorite crackers.
YIELD: 6 to 8 servings for appetizers.

Asparagus Roll-Ups

3 oz. bleu cheese, crumbled
1 (8 oz.) pkg. cream cheese,
   softened (may use nonfat)
1 egg
20 slices Pepperidge Farm
   thin-sliced bread

1 (10 oz.) pkg. frozen asparagus
   spears, cooked
1/2 lb. margarine or butter
Toothpicks

BLEND cheeses with egg.
REMOVE crusts from bread. Flatten bread with rolling pin.
SPREAD each slide with cheese mixture. Place 1 cooked asparagus spear on each slice and roll bread around it; secure with toothpick if necessary. Dip each into melted margarine. Slice into thirds and place on baking sheet.
BAKE in preheated oven at 400° for 15 minutes.
MAY be frozen, thawed, sliced and then baked.
YIELD: 60 pieces.

Bacon-Mushroom Puffs

1/4 c. diced, raw bacon
1 1/2 c. coarsely-chopped
   mushrooms
2 tsp. dried parsley

1 T. lemon juice
2 tsp. all-purpose flour
1/8 tsp. black pepper

IN a heavy skillet, sauté bacon until crisp; remove with slotted spoon, leaving 2 tablespoons of drippings. Drain bacon on paper towels and set aside.
IN pan drippings, sauté mushrooms 2 to 3 minutes. Stir in parsley, lemon juice, all-purpose flour and pepper.
ADD bacon.
SERVE in precooked small puff pastry shells.
YIELD: 4 dozen.

Appetizers

Black Bean Dip

2 (8 oz.) pkg. cream cheese
   softened
1 (10 1/2 oz.) can condensed
   black bean soup, undiluted
1/2 tsp. oregano

1 tsp. grated onion
1 tsp. salt
2 T. Worcestershire sauce
1 tsp. lemon juice
1/8 tsp. chili powder

COMBINE all ingredients; beat with a spoon or in a blender.
YIELD: about 2 1/2 cups.
NOTE: Taste for flavor. Add more oregano, if desired. You could also add more chili powder if needed. If condensed soup is too thick, use a little sour cream to desired consistency. Serve with your choice of chips or crackers.

Bleu Cheese Ball

1 (8 oz.) pkg. cream cheese
4 oz. shredded Cheddar cheese
4 oz. crumbled bleu cheese

2 T. minced onion
Dash of Worcestershire sauce
Chopped nuts

BLEND all ingredients, except nuts.
ROLL into ball; refrigerate.
BEFORE serving, cover with chopped nuts.
SERVE with crackers.
IT is best to make this the day before you are going to serve.

Bourbon Paté

1 1/2 lb. liverwurst
1 c. butter or margarine
1/4 c. bourbon
1/2 tsp. pepper
1/2 c. chopped pitted ripe olives

LET liverwurst and butter or margarine stand at room temperature until soft enough to mash (about 1 hour).
MASH liverwurst with a fork until free of lumps.
ADD butter or margarine and mix well.
ADD bourbon, pepper and black olives; mix thoroughly.
PACK into a mold or small crock that has been lightly oiled; chill several hours.
UNMOLD onto plate, or serve in crock with crackers or toast rounds.
YIELD: 6 servings.

Broiled Shrimp Appetizers

1 1/2 lb. lg. raw shrimp
1/2 c. olive oil
1/4 c. dry sherry
2 lg. cloves, minced
1/8 c. dried parsley
3/4 tsp. salt
1/2 tsp. ground black pepper
1/4 tsp. dried thyme
1/8 tsp. dried red hot peppers
(opt.)

SHELL and devein shrimp, leaving tail shells on.
COMBINE remaining ingredients in a bowl. Add shrimp and allow to stand at room temperature for 1 hour, or 2 hours or more in refrigerator; turn occasionally.
PREHEAT broiler. Arrange shrimp in marinade in a single layer in a shallow broiling pan.
BROIL 6 inches from heat, just until shrimp turn pink and lose translucence, about 4 minutes on each side.
SERVE hot, with marinade spooned over.
YIELD: 18 to 20 appetizer servings.

Appetizers

Caviar Dip

1/2 c. whipping cream	3 hard-boiled eggs, sliced
2 to 3 T. caviar	Toast
1 to 2 T. finely-chopped onions	

WHIP the whipping cream. Fold in caviar and onions.
PLACE in center of dish.
GARNISH with sliced hard-boiled eggs and small rounds of toast.

Caviar Pie

1 med. ctn. small egg black caviar	1 med. onion, finely chopped
1 doz. eggs, hard-boiled	1 stick unsalted butter, melted
	1 (16 oz.) ctn. sour cream

Combine chopped egg, chopped onion and melted butter.
SPREAD mixture on the platter you will be serving on and refrigerate.
EMPTY jar of caviar into a fine-mesh strainer and drain thoroughly.
WHEN mixture is completely chilled (2 hours), spread sour cream on top of egg mixture, leaving some egg exposed on the outer edge to give the illusion of crust.
AFTER making sure caviar is drained completely, spread gently on top of the sour cream, again leaving an edge of sour cream showing.
SERVE with any unsalted cracker or water biscuit.

Cherry Olives

From Ione Schneckloth, my husband's mother, a great cook and a great mother-in-law.

1 qt. water	1/2 c. sugar
1 1/4 c. vinegar	3 T. salt

PACK cherries (bing cherries seem best for this).
POUR pickling mixture over cherries, cold.
SEAL jars tightly and wait about 4 weeks before eating.

Chicken Nuggets and Honey Mustard Sauce

1 c. flour	1 tsp. ground mustard
4 tsp. seasoned salt	1/2 tsp. pepper
1 tsp. paprika	8 boneless chicken breast halves
1 tsp. poultry seasoning	1/4 c. vegetable or olive oil

IN plastic bag, combine the first 6 ingredients.
POUND chicken to 1/2-inch thickness and cut into 1 1/2-inch pieces; shake bag to coat.
HEAT oil in skillet. Cook chicken, turning frequently until brown, 6 to 8 minutes.

HONEY MUSTARD DIP:

1/2 c. mayonnaise	2 T. Dijon mustard
1/2 c. sour cream	2 T. honey

MIX all ingredients in bowl.
CHILL until serving time.
DRESSING may also be used on tossed salad.

Chutney Cheese Paté

6 oz. softened cream cheese	1/2 c. finely-chopped mango
1 c. shredded sharp Cheddar	chutney, or your choice
cheese	3 to 4 green onions, with part
2 T. dry sherry	of green tops, minced
3/4 tsp. curry powder	Crisp sesame wafers of wheat
1/4 tsp. salt	crackers
Dash of Tabasco	

BEAT together cream cheese, Cheddar cheese, sherry, curry powder, salt and Tabasco until almost smooth.
SPREAD on a serving platter, shaping a layer about 1/2-inch thick; leave room around the edge for crackers.
CHILL until firm.
SPREAD chutney on top at serving.
YIELD: 6 to 8 servings.

Appetizers

Crabmeat Quiche

2 (7 1/2 oz.) cans crabmeat
2 c. coarsely-grated Swiss
    cheese
1 (10 oz.) pkg. pie crust mix
6 eggs

1/2 tsp. pepper
3 c. light cream
1/2 c. dry sherry
1 T. salt
1 tsp. nutmeg

CHECK cans of crabmeat and discard any bits of shell.

FLAKE the crabmeat and toss lightly with 2 cups Swiss cheese; set aside.

PREPARE the pie crust mix and roll out on a lightly-floured surface to a 12x18-inch rectangle.

FIT into a 10 1/2 x 15 1/2 x 1-inch jellyroll pan.

SPOON combined crabmeat and cheese into crust.

COMBINE eggs, light cream, dry sherry, salt, nutmeg and pepper; beat well.

POUR over crabmeat mixture in pie crust and bake for 15 minutes at 425°.

REDUCE heat to 325° and bake 20 to 30 minutes more, or until knife inserted in center comes out clean.

SERVE warm.

CUT into 1x2-inch rectangles.

YIELD: 150 pieces.

Cranberry Meat Balls

2 lb. ground beef
1 c. cornflake crumbs
1/3 c. dried parsley
2 eggs
2 T. soy sauce

1/4 tsp. pepper
1/2 tsp. garlic salt
1/3 c. ketchup
2 T. dried minced onion

BLEND above ingredients; form into 50¢-size balls.
COVER bottom of 10x15-inch baking dish with the meat balls.

SAUCE:
2 T. brown sugar
1 (1 lb.) can whole
    cranberry sauce

2 T. lemon juice
1 (12 oz.) jar chili sauce

COOK and stir over medium heat until smooth.
POUR over meat balls.
BAKE at 350° for 30 minutes in a preheated oven.
YIELD: 20 to 25 small meat balls for appetizers.

Cranberry Salsa

1 (16 oz.) can Ocean Spray
    whole-berry cranberry
    sauce
1/4 c. canned jalapeños,
    chopped

1 green onion, sliced
1 tsp. dried cilantro
1 tsp. ground cumin
1 tsp. lime juice

COMBINE all ingredients in a medium bowl.
SERVE with nacho chips or as a condiment for poultry or pork.
STORE in refrigerator in a tightly-sealed container, up to 3 weeks.
YIELD: 2 cups.

Appetizers

Cream Cheese Covered by
Cranberry Chutney

2 c. fresh or frozen cranberries   1 tsp. salt
2 sm. tomatoes, peeled,   1 c. packed brown sugar
    seeded & coarsely chopped   1/2 c. cider vinegar
    (3/4 c.)   1/2 tsp. ground ginger
1/2 c. light raisins   1/2 tsp. ground cloves
1/4 c. minced onions   1/2 tsp. pepper
3/4 c. water

IN a 3-quart saucepan, combine cranberries, tomatoes, water, raisins, onions and salt. Bring to boiling.
SIMMER, covered, 15 minutes or until cranberries pop.
STIR in brown sugar, vinegar, ginger, cloves and pepper.
COVER; cook 35 to 40 minutes or until the consistency of relish, stirring occasionally.
LADLE into jars or freezer containers.
REFRIGERATE or freeze.
YIELD: 2 2/3 cups.

FOR APPETIZERS, WITH CRANBERRY CHUTNEY:
1 or 2 (8 oz.) pkg. softened   Chilled cranberry chutney
    cream cheese

PLACE softened cream cheese on serving plate.
COVER with cranberry chutney, amount may vary to taste.
ARRANGE with crackers surrounding mounds. Place small serving knife on side to allow guests to serve themselves.

THIS recipe may be varied in any number of ways. You could use mint jelly, orange marmalade, lemon curd, and many other possibilities to change the colors, or atmosphere you desire.

Appetizers   9

Hot Crab Special

6 oz. king crabmeat
1 (8 oz.) pkg. cream cheese
2 T. finely-chopped onions
2 T. milk

1/2 tsp. cream-style horseradish
1/4 tsp. salt
1/3 c. toasted almonds (opt.)

COMBINE all ingredients except almonds, mixing until well blended.
SPOON mixture into 8-inch pie pan.
SPRINKLE almonds on top.
BAKE at 375° for 15 minutes.
SERVE with assorted crackers or party round breads.
YIELD: 6 to 8 appetizer servings.

Hot Deviled Shrimp

1 (12 oz.) pkg. frozen
   deveined shrimp, or
   1 1/2 c. cooked fresh
   shrimp
4 T. butter or margarine
1 tsp. Worcestershire sauce

1 tsp. curry powder
1/2 tsp. Tabasco
1/2 tsp. salt
1/4 tsp. pepper
1/2 tsp. celery salt

BREAK shrimp apart; let partially defrost.
MELT butter or margarine in chafing dish over direct heat.
STIR in Worcestershire sauce and curry powder; continue to stir until very hot. Add remaining ingredients and mix well.
ADD shrimp; sauté about 5 minutes, until cooked and well-seasoned with butter mixture.
SERVE hot.
YIELD: 8 appetizer servings. (These look good served in a scallop shell, or other seafood shell.)

Hot Spinach Balls

3 pkg. frozen spinach,   9 eggs
   cooked & chopped   2 onions, chopped
1 (1 lb.) bag Pepperidge Farm 1 c. margarine, melted
   herb stuffing   2 tsp. garlic powder
1 lb. Mozzarella cheese, grated 1 tsp. black pepper

MIX all ingredients to form small balls. Place on cookie sheet and freeze.
AFTER frozen, place in plastic bag until needed.
BAKE, frozen, in preheated 375° oven for 20 minutes.

Icicle Pickles

This is a recipe from my husband's grandmother, Frieda Hoffmann.

1 gal. whole med. to sm.   Celery stalks, small, or chopped
   cucumbers (est.)   2 to 4 c. sliced onions
4 c. vinegar   Dill (fresh, or 1 tsp. dried)
4 c. sugar   1/4 tsp. alum
2 c. water   8 to 10 garlic cloves
1/2 c. salt

PLACE whole pickles in ice water for 2 hours.
PLACE celery, onion, garlic, dill and alum in each jar.
BRING vinegar, sugar, salt and water to a boil. Add drained cucumbers to each jar and cover with syrup.
ADD a clove to each jar and seal tightly.

Jitney Pickles

This recipe is from my mother-in-law, Ione Schneckloth. She always seems to make these and other great recipes with great ease.

4 qt. sliced cucumbers (average)	2 c. sugar
1 "good" handful salt (1/2 c.)	1 c. vinegar
2 T. mustard seed	Celery seed, to taste (1 tsp.)
1 gal. boiling water	2 drops oil of cloves
	2 drops oil of cinnamon

MIX boiling water, salt and mustard seed; pour over sliced cucumbers. Let stand until cold.
DRAIN.
COMBINE sugar, vinegar, celery seed, oil of cloves and oil of cinnamon in a large saucepan; bring to a boil.
ADD cucumbers and let mixture come to a "good" boil.
REMOVE from heat and pack in jars; seal tightly.

Marinated Shrimp

1 lb. cooked shrimp, butterflied & well drained	Bay leaf
	3 lg. garlic cloves, crushed
4 T. water	1 tsp. basil
4 T. lemon juice	1 tsp. rosemary
4 T. barbecue sauce of your choice	1 tsp. paprika
	2 tsp. red chili powder (hot, med., or mild)
1/2 tsp. salt	
1 tsp. pepper	

MARINATE 4 hours or more.
SIMMER 5 minutes or until warm; remove bay leaf.
SERVE hot, in sauce, with toothpicks.
YIELD: 8 to 10 servings as appetizers.

Phyllo-Spinach Appetizers

1/2 pkg. phyllo dough
1/2 stick butter or margarine
3 eggs
1 c. flour
1 c. milk

1 tsp. salt
1 tsp. baking powder
1 lb. grated Monterey Jack cheese
1 pkg. frozen spinach, thawed &
   well drained

MELT butter in pan.
PUT 4 sheets of phyllo dough in a 9x13-inch pan.
BEAT eggs; add rest of ingredients. Mix well and pour into the
prepared pan.
PLACE 4 additional sheets of phyllo dough over the mixture.
BRUSH dough with a little melted butter.
BAKE at 350° for 35 minutes.
COOL for 30 minutes and cut into small squares.
YIELD: 12 servings.

Pineapple-Mint Jam

3 1/2 c. (1 lb. 13 oz. can)
   crushed pineapple
3/4 c. water
Juice of 2 lemons

7 1/2 c. sugar
1 (6 oz.) btl. liquid pectin
1 tsp. peppermint extract
Green food coloring

MIX the first 4 ingredients.
BRING to a boil, stirring.
BOIL for 2 minutes.
ADD pectin, peppermint, and coloring to desired tint.
STIR and skim foam for 5 minutes.
POUR into hot sterilized jars and seal.
YIELD: 5 (1/2-pint) jars.

Port-Cheddar Spread

1 (13 1/4 oz.) can crushed pineapple, drained well	2 tsp. finely-chopped onions
8 oz. cream cheese, softened	1 T. seasoned salt
2 c. shredded Cheddar cheese	1 tsp. garlic powder
1/3 c. port wine	1/4 tsp. dry mustard
	1 T. dried parsley

DRAIN pincapple well; beat softened cream cheese with Cheddar cheese and wine until smooth.

BEAT in seasoned salt, garlic powder and mustard.

FOLD in parsley and drained pineapple.

SPOON into a small crock and chill well before serving.

YIELD: 3 cups.

THIS spread is very pretty, and has a great flavor. Serve on your favorite cracker or party bread.

Raspberry Cheese Torte

1 1/2 lb. Cheddar cheese,
   grated
1/4 c. finely-minced onion
3/4 c. chopped pecans
1/4 tsp. cayenne pepper
Fresh raspberries

Assorted crackers (unflavored)
1/3 to 1/2 c. Hellmann's
   mayonnaise
1/4 to 1/2 tsp. hot pepper sauce
1 c. good quality raspberry
   preserves

PLACE grated cheese in a large bowl and let stand at room temperature until soft and slightly oily.
STIR in pecans, cayenne, mayonnaise and pepper sauce.
KNEAD with hands until well blended.
LINE a 10-inch flan pan with plastic wrap.
PRESS cheese mixture firmly into pan.
COVER with additional plastic wrap and press mixture again to mold firmly.
REFRIGERATE at least 4 hours, or until cheese is firm again.
TO serve, unmold torte onto serving dish.
SPREAD top with preserves, and garnish with fresh raspberries or a lemon rose.
SERVE with assorted crackers.
YIELD: 15 to 20 appetizer servings.

Red-Pepper Jam

WASH and seed 1 dozen large sweet red peppers.
CHOP finely in a food processor.
ADD 1 tablespoon salt and let stand overnight.
DRAIN well, pressing out all liquid.
PLACE in a kettle with 2 cups white vinegar and 3 cups sugar.
COOK, uncovered, for 45 minutes, or until of marmalade consistency, stirring frequently.
POUR in hot sterilized jars and seal.
YIELD: 4 to 5 (1/2-pint) jars.

Sausage-Stuffed Mushrooms

1 lb. bulk sausage
1 (8 oz.) pkg. cream cheese,
   softened
1/2 c. chopped onions

1 clove garlic, chopped
1 or 2 pkg. fresh mushrooms,
   med. to lg. size
Drop of olive oil

BROWN sausage until crumbled and cooked; drain and set aside.
IN a large skillet with olive oil, lightly brown onions over medium heat.
ADD in cream cheese, sausage and garlic; mix well, over low heat, until mixture is of good consistency.
PREPARE mushrooms by wiping with a paper towel and popping off stems. You may save stems, chop and add to stuffing mixture.
LAY mushrooms on foil-covered baking sheet and stuff with mixture. Top with Parmesan or Romano cheese.
BAKE at 425° for 15 to 25 minutes.

Sautéed Cauliflowerets

2 1/2 c. cauliflowerets
   (1 med. head)
1 c. butter or margarine
1 clove garlic, crushed

1 1/2 tsp. bottled garlic salt with
   parsley
1 1/2 tsp. lemon pepper

BREAK medium head cauliflower into bite-size flowerets, to make 2 1/2 cups.
WASH and dry thoroughly.
IN a large skillet, melt 1 cup butter or margarine and add 1 garlic clove, crushed.
ADD cauliflowerets and sauté gently 10 or 15 minutes, or until tender but still crisp. Drain on paper towels.
COMBINE 1 1/2 teaspoons, each, bottled garlic salt with parsley, and lemon pepper; sprinkle over cauliflower. Serve warm.
CAULIFLOWERETS may be kept for up to 30 minutes in a 300° oven and still remain crisp.
YIELD: about 3 cups.

NOTE: You may use 2 (10-ounce) bags frozen cauliflower, thawed and dried thoroughly with paper towels.

Appetizers

Shrimp Ball

1 (8 oz.) pkg. cream cheese, softened	1 tsp. seasoned salt
	1/2 tsp. horseradish mustard
1/2 tsp. garlic powder	1 c. shrimp, cooked & chopped
2 T. chopped stuffed olives	1/2 tsp. onion powder
3 tsp. lemon juice	Pecans, finely chopped

MIX all ingredients (except pecans), together thoroughly.

SHAPE into a ball, then roll in enough chopped pecans to cover completely.

CHILL several hours or overnight, before serving with crackers or chips of your choice.

Shrimp-in-a-Blanket

36 shrimp, shelled & deveined	18 slices bacon, cut in half
1/3 c. prepared mustard of your choice (I use Dijon)	

WASH and dry thoroughly the 36 shrimp.

SPREAD each of the 18 bacon slices, cut in half, with about 1/2 teaspoon of the prepared mustard.

WRAP the shrimp in a prepared, halved bacon slice and secure with a toothpick.

PREHEAT broiler for 5 minutes. Broil shrimp 6 inches from heat for 3 to 4 minutes. Turn and broil 2 or 3 minutes longer.

SERVE hot.

YIELD: 36 shrimp wrapped in bacon.

Smoked Turkey Dip

1/4 c. chopped onion
1 T. margarine
1 (8 oz.) pkg. cream cheese, cubed
1 (2 1/2 oz.) pkg. smoked
  turkey, chopped

1 (4 oz.) can mushrooms, drained
1/4 c. grated Parmesan cheese
1 T. dried parsley
French bread

SAUTÉ onion in margarine; add milk and cheese.
STIR over low heat until cream cheese is melted; stir in remaining
ingredients and heat thoroughly.
SERVE hot with toasted French bread slices.

Spinach Dip

1 (10 oz.) pkg. frozen
  spinach
1 c. mayonnaise
1 env. Knorr vegetable soup
  mix

1 c. sour cream
1 (8 1/2 oz.) can water
  chestnuts, chopped
1/2 sm. onion, minced

THAW spinach completely, then squeeze all the water out.
MIX spinach with the other ingredients and blend well.
REFRIGERATE overnight, before serving with crackers or chips.

Stuffed Mild Jalapeños

8 oz. Hellmann's real
mayonnaise
12 oz. bacon, cooked crisp &
crumbled
2 sm. bunches green onion,
chopped

8 oz. sharp Cheddar cheese,
grated
10 oz. chopped pecans or
almonds
2 (12 oz.) cans mild jalapeño
halves

DRAIN jalapeños; rinse and pat dry.
MIX all remaining ingredients; stuff jalapeños.
REFRIGERATE until ready to serve.
YIELD: 10 to 12 appetizer servings.

Stuffed Mushrooms

12 med. to lg. mushrooms
1 tsp. minced onion
1 can crabmeat

1/4 c. shredded cabbage
1 c. fine cracker crumbs
6 strips bacon, cut in half

STEM and wash mushrooms; save stems for stuffing.
MIX remainder of ingredients and fill each mushroom.
WRAP each with a bacon strip; secure with a toothpick.
BAKE for 30 minutes on a shallow pan, at 375°.

Stuffed Mushrooms

8 oz. cream cheese
1/2 stick margarine
1/2 c. bread crumbs
1/2 tsp. salt
1/2 tsp. pepper
1/2 c. grated Parmesan cheese
1/2 c. bacon bits

1 lg. pkg. mushrooms with
    stems, from produce dept.
1/4 tsp. garlic powder
1 T. chopped onion
2 to 4 T. sherry
3 to 4 tsp. Worcestershire sauce

MIX cream cheese, garlic and Worcestershire sauce; set aside.
POP stems from caps of mushrooms. Rinse stems and caps. Chop stems very finely; add to cream cheese mixture.
MELT 4 tablespoons butter; let cool a little and coat the mushroom caps.
MIX cream cheese mixture, bread crumbs, onion, salt, pepper, bacon bits, half of Parmesan cheese and sherry; fill mushroom caps with mixture.
GENEROUSLY butter a shallow baking dish; place stuffed mushrooms in dish.
MELT remaining butter.
SPRINKLE Parmesan cheese on each cap; drizzle with melted butter.
BAKE at 350° for about 25 minutes. (Make sure juice is in the bottom dish before you remove from the oven. If not, bake a little longer until there is some juice in the pan.)

Appetizers

Swedish Meat Balls
(Microwave)

1 lb. ground beef	1/2 tsp. salt
1 egg	1/8 tsp. allspice
1/2 c. dry bread crumbs	1/8 tsp. pepper
1/2 c. milk, divided	1 (10 3/4 oz.) can condensed
1 sm. onion, finely chopped	golden mushroom soup
2 tsp. parsley flakes	

COMBINE ground beef, egg, bread crumbs, 1/4 cup of the milk, onion, parsley, salt, allspice and pepper.

SHAPE into 1 1/4-inch meat balls (about 20).

ARRANGE in an 8-inch square baking dish; cover with waxed paper.

COOK at medium for 9 to 10 minutes.

IN a small bowl, blend soup and remaining milk; combine with meat balls.

COOK, covered, at HIGH, 14 minutes, or until heated through.

YIELD: 20 medium-size, or 35 smaller meat balls.

Sweet and Sour Meat Balls

1 lb. ground beef	1/2 c. sugar
1 1/2 tsp. salt	1/4 c. wine vinegar
1/2 tsp. pepper	2 T. soy sauce
1 (5 oz.) can water chestnuts	1 med. green pepper, chopped
finely sliced	in 1/2" pieces
1 c. milk	1/2 c. celery, chopped in 1/2"
1/4 c. flour	pieces
1/2 c. butter	1 sm. can pineapple chunks or
2 T. cornstarch	tidbits, with juice

COMBINE beef, seasonings, water chestnuts and milk. Work and form into small balls. Roll in flour and fry in butter over medium heat until brown and well done.

COMBINE remaining ingredients in saucepan and bring to a boil; reduce heat and simmer for 3 minutes.

POUR over meat balls and serve in chafing dish.

YIELD: 20 appetizer servings.

Appetizers

Sweet and Spicy Almonds

1 c. sliced almonds	1/4 tsp. chili powder
1 T. butter or margarine, melted	1/8 tsp. dried, crushed red pepper
	1/4 tsp. ground cumin
1 1/2 tsp. sugar	Pinch of salt

COMBINE almonds and butter, stirring well. Combine sugar and remaining ingredients.

SPRINKLE over almonds; toss to coat.

SPREAD on a lightly-greased baking sheet.

BAKE at 325°, stirring occasionally, 15 minutes; cool.

YIELD: 1 cup.

Veggie Squares

2 pkg. crescent rolls	3/4 c. tomatoes, finely chopped
2 (8 oz.) pkg. cream cheese	3/4 c. green peppers, finely chopped
3/4 c. mayonnaise	
1 pkg. Hidden Valley Ranch dressing mix	1/2 c. onion, finely chopped
	1/2 c. cauliflower
3/4 c. broccoli, finely chopped	1/2 c. cheese, grated

SPREAD crescent rolls flat on baking sheet. Bake at 350° for 8 to 10 minutes and let cool.

CREAM together cream cheese, mayonnaise and ranch dressing mix; spread on cooled crescent rolls.

COVER with finely-chopped vegetables and cheese.

CUT into 2-inch squares.

YIELD: 15 to 20 appetizer servings.

BREAKFAST AND BREADS

List Your Favorite Recipes

Recipes   **Page**

_____   _____

_____   _____

_____   _____

_____   _____

_____   _____

_____   _____

_____   _____

_____   _____

_____   _____

_____   _____

_____   _____

_____   _____

_____   _____

_____   _____

_____   _____

_____   _____

_____   _____

_____   _____

Apple Pancakes

1 c. flour	1 T. vegetable oil
1 T. sugar	2 lg. apples, peeled & chopped
1/2 tsp. salt	Powdered sugar (opt.)
1 egg	1 tsp. cinnamon & 4 T. sugar,
1 c. milk	mixed (opt.)

IN a bowl, combine flour, sugar and salt. Set aside.
IN another bowl, lightly beat egg; add milk and oil.
ADD dry ingredients and stir until smooth.
PEEL and finely chop apples.
POUR batter, 1/2 cup at a time, onto lightly-greased griddle; sprinkle apples on each, and turn when bubbles form.
COOK on second side until golden and apples are tender.
SERVE sprinkled with powdered sugar, or cinnamon and sugar and maple syrup.

Breakfast Enchiladas

1 lb. ground fully-cooked ham	1 T. flour
1/2 c. green onions, sliced	1/4 tsp. salt
1/2 c. green pepper, chopped	1/4 tsp. garlic powder
8 (7") flour tortillas	A few drops Tabasco sauce
4 eggs, beaten	Cheddar cheese
2 c. milk	

IN a bowl, combine ham, onion and green pepper.
PLACE 1/3 cup of mixture and 3 tablespoons shredded Cheddar cheese in each tortilla.
ROLL up and arrange, seam-side down, on a greased 7 1/2 x 12-inch baking dish.
COMBINE eggs, milk, flour, salt, garlic powder and Tabasco.
POUR over tortillas; cover and refrigerate several hours, or overnight.
BAKE, uncovered, in a 250° oven for 45 to 50 minutes; sprinkle with Cheddar cheese and bake a few more minutes, until cheese melts.
LET stand 10 minutes before serving.
YIELD: 8 servings.

Caramel Twists

SWEET DOUGH:
4 1/2 c. sifted all-purpose flour
1/4 c. sugar
1 tsp. salt
3 egg yolks, beaten

3/4 c. butter or margarine
1 pkg. active dry yeast
1/4 c. warm water
1 c. milk, scalded & cooled to
   lukewarm

MIX flour, sugar and salt; cut in butter until size of small peas. Set aside.
DISSOLVE yeast in warm water; add to flour mixture along with beaten egg yolks and milk.
BEAT until thoroughly mixed and smooth.
COVER and chill overnight.

CARAMEL COATING:
2/3 c. butter or margarine
1/4 c. light corn syrup

1 1/2 c. packed brown sugar
1 c. chopped walnuts

WHEN ready to bake, prepare coating by melting butter in a small saucepan.
STIR in syrup; spread in the bottom of 2 (10 x 15 x 1 1/2-inch) jellyroll pans.
SPRINKLE 2/3 cup of the brown sugar and 1/2 cup of the nuts evenly in each pan.

FILLING:
1/2 c. brown sugar

1 tsp. cinnamon

MIX the filling; divide in thirds.
CUT the dough into three equal parts for easy handling.
ROLL each third of dough into a rectangle, 15x10 inches.
BRUSH center third of 15-inch side of one rectangle with soft butter; sprinkle with filling mixture.
FOLD one-third of rectangle over center third, and sprinkle with filling mixture. Fold remaining third over the other 2 layers.
CUT crosswise into 1-inch-wide strips.
GRASP ends and twist; seal ends firmly in fan shape.
PLACE dough strips in pan, 1 inch apart.
REPEAT with remaining 2 parts of dough to fill 2 pans.
ALLOW to rise 1/2 hour in warm place, free from draft.
BAKE in 350° oven 25 minutes.
INVERT pans immediately onto large sheets of foil.
ALLOW pans to remain inverted for 1 minute before removing pan.

Breakfast and Breads

Christmas Morning Strata

1 lb. ground pork sausage
2 tsp. prepared mustard
6 slices white sandwich
    bread, crusts removed
2 c. (8 oz.) shredded Swiss cheese

1 1/2 c. milk
3 lg. eggs, lightly beaten
1/2 tsp. Worcestershire sauce
1/8 tsp. salt
1/8 tsp. ground nutmeg

BROWN sausage in a skillet over medium heat, stirring until it crumbles; drain well. Stir in mustard.
FIT bread into a greased 7 x 11 x 1 1/2-inch baking dish; top with sausage mixture and cheese.
COMBINE milk and next 5 ingredients; pour over bread mixture. Cover and refrigerate 8 hours.
BAKE, uncovered, at 350° for 50 minutes, or until set.
YIELD: 6 servings.

Cinnamon-Sugar French Toast

1/4 c. sugar
1 tsp. cinnamon
4 slices sourdough bread,
    1/2" thick
4 eggs, well beaten

Vegetable oil
Confectioners' sugar (opt.)
Butter
Maple syrup, warm

MIX sugar and cinnamon; set aside.
CUT bread slices in half diagonally.
DIP in beaten eggs, soaking bread well with egg.
HEAT oil in a skillet and fry bread, turning to brown both sides.
ROLL once in sugar and cinnamon, and dust with confectioners' sugar, if desired.
SERVE with butter and syrup.
YIELD: 4 servings.

YOU CAN VARY THIS RECIPE:
ADD 1 cup of milk to eggs (use only 2 eggs).
USE 1/2 teaspoon sugar and 1 1/2 teaspoons cinnamon, and add to milk/egg mixture.
SLICE the sourdough bread 3/4-inch thick.
REMOVE from pan and roll in confectioners' sugar.

Coconut Buns

3 1/2 c. flour	1 c. butter
1/2 c. sugar	3 eggs
2 tsp. baking powder	3/4 c. milk
1/2 tsp. salt	1 c. raisins
2 T. lemon extract or lemon rind	1 1/4 c. shredded coconut
	2 egg whites, lightly beaten

IN a large mixing bowl, combine flour, sugar, baking powder, salt and lemon rind.

CUT in butter until mixture is crumbly in texture.

BEAT eggs with milk and add to flour mixture.

BLEND just until moistened.

ADD raisins and coconut; mix again, just enough to incorporate. Do not overmix.

USING an ice cream scoop or tablespoon, drop dough onto a greased cookie sheet.

BRUSH the tops of each bun with egg whites and sprinkle with sugar.

BAKE in preheated 350° oven for 25 minutes, or until firm.

YIELD: 2 dozen.

Cranberry Orange Pound Cake
with Butter Almond Sauce

1 box Duncan Hines Orange Supreme cake mix
3 eggs
1/3 c. oil
1 c. chopped cranberries
1 box instant vanilla pudding

PREHEAT oven to 350°.
GREASE and flour bundt pan.
BLEND cake mix, water, oil and eggs in a large bowl, on slow speed, until moistened.
BEAT at medium speed for 2 minutes.
FOLD in vanilla pudding and cranberries.
POUR into prepared pan.
BAKE for 50 to 55 minutes.
COOL in pan on wire rack for 15 minutes.
REMOVE from pan and cool.

BUTTER ALMOND SAUCE:
1 sm. can evaporated milk
1 stick butter
1 c. sugar
1 T. flour
1 tsp. almond extract

MIX milk, butter, sugar and flour with whisk over medium-high heat.
BRING to a boil; turn to low and immediately add almond extract.
SERVE 2 tablespoons of the warm sauce over a slice of the cake.

Cranberry Scones

2 1/2 c. all-purpose flour
1/2 c. sugar
2 tsp. baking powder
1/2 tsp. salt
1/2 tsp. ground cloves

1/4 c. butter or margarine
1 c. whipping cream
3/4 c. fresh or frozen
  cranberries, coarsely
  chopped

COMBINE the first 5 ingredients; cut in butter with a pastry blender until mixture is crumbly.

RESERVE 1 tablespoon whipping cream; add remaining whipping cream and cranberries to flour mixture, stirring just until moistened.

TURN dough out onto a lightly-floured surface; knead 5 or 6 times. Shape into an 8-inch circle. Cut into 8 wedges; place on a lightly-greased baking sheet. Prick wedges with a fork 3 or 4 times, and brush with reserved 1 tablespoon whipping cream.

BAKE at 425° for 18 minutes, or until lightly browned. Serve warm, with whipped cream, if desired.

YIELD: 8 servings.

Croissants

1 c. butter, softened	2/3 c. milk
2 env. active dry yeast	4 to 4 1/2 c. all-purpose flour divided
3 T. sugar, divided	1/4 c. vegetable oil
1/2 c. warm water	2 tsp. salt

PRESS batter into a 10x8-inch rectangle on waxed paper; chill.

COMBINE yeast, 1 tablespoon sugar and water in a 2-cup liquid measuring cup; let stand 5 minutes.

HEAT milk to 105° to 115°. Combine yeast mixture, warm milk, remaining 2 tablespoons sugar, 2 cups flour and next 3 ingredients in a large mixing bowl. Beat mixture at medium speed with an electric mixer until smooth. Gradually stir in enough remaining flour to make a soft dough.

TURN dough out onto a floured surface; knead until smooth and elastic, about 10 minutes. Place in well-greased bowl, turning to grease top.

COVER and let rise in a warm place (85°), free from drafts, 1 hour, or until dough has doubled in bulk.

PUNCH dough down. Cover with plastic wrap and chill dough 1 hour.

PUNCH dough down; turn out onto a lightly-floured surface and roll into a 24x10-inch rectangle. Place chilled butter rectangle in center of dough rectangle; carefully fold dough over butter. Pinch edges to seal.

ROLL dough into an 18x10-inch rectangle; fold into thirds, beginning with short side. Cover and chill 1 hour.

REPEAT rolling and folding procedure twice, chilling dough 30 minutes each time. Wrap dough in aluminum foil and chill 8 hours.

DIVIDE dough into 4 equal portions. Roll 1 portion into 12-inch circle on lightly-floured surface; cut in 6 wedges (keep remaining dough chilled). Roll up each wedge tightly, beginning at wide end. Place, point-side down, on greased baking sheets, gently curving rolls into crescent shapes. Cover; let rise in a warm place, free from drafts, 30 minutes, or until doubled in bulk.

BAKE at 425° for 8 minutes, or until lightly golden. Cool croissants slightly on baking sheets, and transfer to wire racks to cool. Repeat procedure with remaining dough portions.

YIELD: 2 dozen.

Continued on following page.

Continued from preceding page.

CHOCOLATE-FILLED CROISSANTS: Place 2 or 3 tiny rectangles of a milk chocolate candy bar on the wide end of each croissant dough wedge, and roll up each wedge. Proceed as directed in recipe.
STRAWBERRY OR APRICOT CROISSANTS: Spread 1 table-spoon strawberry or apricot preserves evenly over each dough wedge, leaving a 1/4-inch border; roll up and proceed as directed in recipe.
CINNAMON AND SUGAR: Sprinkle wedges evenly with mixture of ground cinnamon and sugar; roll up and proceed as directed in recipe. Drizzle with icing of milk and powdered sugar. Drizzle over top of croissants.

Focaccia

1 pt. warm water	2 lb. (about 8 c.) high-gluten
1 cake yeast (in refrigerated	flour (may use bread flour)
section)	1/4 to 3/8 c. freshly-grated
1/8 c. sugar	Parmesan cheese
1 T. table salt	1 T. kosher salt
Extra-virgin olive oil	1/8 c. fresh rosemary leaves

PLACE water in a mixing bowl and stir in yeast; let stand 5 minutes, or until it is bubbly.
ADD sugar, table salt and 1/2 cup oil; mix until incorporated.
POUR mixture into large bowl of electric mixer and add flour. Mix gently with dough hook 5 to 6 minutes, or until fully incorporated (Dough should not be sticky or too dry).
PLACE dough in oiled bowl; cover and let rest until double in size, about 30 to 45 minutes.
PUNCH down and roll out to fit 1 (15 1/2 x 10 1/2 x 1-inch) jellyroll pan.
LIGHTLY brush with oil and let rise, uncovered, 30 to 45 minutes.
SPRINKLE with 1/4 cup freshly-grated Parmesan, kosher salt and rosemary. Plunge fingers into the dough to make pockmark indentations all over surface.
BAKE at 400° for 20 to 30 minutes, or until browned on top.
CUT into squares.
SERVE with olive oil, vinegar and Parmesan for dipping.
YIELD: 15 pieces.

Breakfast and Breads

Ham Quiche

3 eggs
1 c. half & half
1/4 tsp. nutmeg
1/2 tsp. salt
1/8 tsp. pepper

1/2 lb. cooked ham, cut into thin strips
2 c. Swiss cheese, shredded
1 baked 9" pastry shell (must be in glass pie pan)

BEAT eggs, cream and seasonings well; stir in ham and cheese.
POUR into baked pie shell.
HEAT, uncovered, in microwave for 5 minutes; move cooked edges toward center and cook 12 minutes more, or until knife inserted in center comes out clean.
LET stand at room temperature 3 to 4 minutes.
SERVE.

WHEN having a brunch, it helps to have the ingredients for this quiche, it is easy and very fast to make if you find yourself running out of food.

Breakfast and Breads

Ham Strata

1 T. butter or margarine
1 c. chopped celery
1/3 c. green bell pepper (opt.)
2 T. chopped onion
2 c. chopped, cooked ham
1/4 c. mayonnaise, divided
12 slices white bread, crusts
   removed

1 (6 oz.) pkg. sharp Cheddar
   cheese slices
4 lg. eggs
3 c. milk
3/4 tsp. salt
1/4 tsp. pepper
Garnishes: sour cream, fresh
   parsley, if desired

MELT butter in a large skillet over medium-high heat.
ADD celery, bell pepper and onion; cook, stirring constantly, until tender.
REMOVE from heat; stir in ham.
COOL.
SPREAD 1 teaspoon mayonnaise on each bread slice.
ARRANGE 6 bread slices, mayonnaise-side up, in a lightly-greased 9x13x2-inch baking dish.
SPOON ham mixture over bread slices; top with cheese and remaining bread, mayonnaise-side down.
COMBINE eggs and next 3 ingredients, stirring well; pour over bread slices.
COVER and refrigerate 8 hours, or overnight.
REMOVE from refrigerator 30 minutes before baking.
BAKE at 300° for 1 1/2 hours.
GARNISH, if desired.
SERVE immediately.
YIELD: 6 servings.

Hash Brown Bake

3 c. frozen, shredded potatoes
1/3 c. butter or margarine,
   melted
1 c. finely-chopped, cooked
   ham
1 c. shredded Cheddar cheese

1/4 c. finely-chopped green
   bell pepper
2 lg. eggs, beaten
1/2 c. milk
1/2 tsp. salt
1/4 tsp. pepper

THAW potatoes between layers of paper towels to remove excess moisture. Press potatoes into bottom and up sides of an ungreased 9-inch pie plate; drizzle with butter.

BAKE at 425° for 25 minutes, or until lightly browned; cool on a wire rack 10 minutes.

COMBINE ham, cheese and bell pepper; spoon into potato shell. Combine next 3 ingredients, stirring well; pour egg mixture over ham mixture.

BAKE at 350° for 25 to 30 minutes, or until set; let stand 10 minutes before serving.

YIELD: 6 to 8 servings.

Herb-Cheese Bread Braid

2 to 2 1/2 c. all-purpose flour	3/4 tsp. dried oregano, crushed
1 pkg. active dry yeast	1/2 tsp. salt
1/4 c. grated Parmesan cheese	2 c. whole wheat flour
1 1/2 c. milk	1 egg
2 T. honey	1 T. water
2 T. butter or margarine	Sesame seeds &/or poppy seeds

IN large mixer bowl, combine 1 1/2 cups all-purpose flour, the yeast and Parmesan cheese.

IN a saucepan, heat milk, honey, butter, oregano and salt until warm (115° to 120°) and butter is almost melted; stir constantly. Add to flour mixture.

BEAT on low speed for 30 seconds; scrape bowl. Beat on high speed for 3 minutes.

USING a spoon, stir in whole wheat flour and as much of the remaining all-purpose flour as you can.

ON lightly-floured surface, knead in enough remaining all-purpose flour to make moderately stiff, smooth, elastic dough, 6 to 8 minutes.

PLACE in a grease bowl; turn once.

COVER and let rise in a warm place until double, about 1 to 1 1/4 hours.

PUNCH down.

DIVIDE in half.

COVER and let rest for 10 minutes.

SHAPE.

COVER and let rise until nearly double, 30 to 45 minutes.

BEAT egg and water lightly; carefully brush over braid.

SPRINKLE with sesame or poppy seeds, or sprinkle alternate twists with sesame and poppy seeds.

BAKE in a 375° oven about 30 minutes, or until bread tests done, covering with foil after 15 minutes, if necessary, to prevent overbrowning.

COOL on wire rack.

YIELD: 1 braid.

Italian Herb Bread

1 c. sour cream	1/3 c. grated Parmesan cheese
1/3 c. milk	1 T. minced onion
3 T. butter, melted	2 tsp. Italian seasoning
2 1/2 c. all-purpose flour	1 egg white, slightly beaten
1 T. sugar	Additional Parmesan cheese &
1 tsp. baking soda	Italian seasoning
1/2 tsp. salt	

PREHEAT oven to 350°.

IN a small bowl, combine sour cream, milk and butter; set aside.

IN a large bowl, combine flour, sugar, baking soda, salt, Parmesan cheese, onion and Italian seasoning.

STIR in sour cream mixture until moistened.

PLACE dough onto a lightly-floured surface; knead until smooth, about 1 minute.

DIVIDE dough into 2 round loaves.

PLACE loaves on greased cookie sheet.

BRUSH tops of loaves with egg white; sprinkle with additional Parmesan cheese and Italian seasoning.

CUT an X about 1/2-inch through top of each loaf.

BAKE 30 to 35 minutes, or until golden brown.

YIELD: 2 loaves.

Kolaches

1 pkg. active dry yeast	3 3/4 to 4 1/2 c. all-purpose
1/4 c. warm water	flour
3/4 c. milk	1/4 tsp. ground cinnamon
1/2 c. butter or margarine	2 eggs
1/4 c. sugar	1 tsp. finely-shredded lemon
1 tsp. salt	peel

IN a bowl, add yeast to water, stirring to dissolve yeast.

IN a saucepan, heat milk, butter or margarine, sugar and salt to just warm, stirring until butter almost melts.

IN a large mixing bowl, stir together 2 cups of the flour and the cinnamon; beat in the milk mixture.

ADD softened yeast, eggs and lemon peel; beat well.

STIR in as much of the remaining flour as you can mix in with a spoon.

TURN out onto a lightly-floured surface.

KNEAD in enough of the remaining flour to make a moderately-soft dough.

CONTINUE kneading until smooth and elastic, 5 minutes.

SHAPE into a ball.

PLACE dough in a lightly-greased bowl; turn once to grease surface.

COVER; let rise until double, 1 to 1 1/2 hours.

PUNCH down; turn out onto lightly-floured surface.

DIVIDE dough into 2 portions.

COVER; let rise in warm place until double, about 45 minutes.

WITH your fingers, make a depression in center of each.

SPOON a heaping tablespoon of the prune or apricot filling evenly into each depression.

BAKE in 375° oven for 12 to 15 minutes, or until golden brown.

REMOVE pastries to a wire rack; cool completely.

DUST pastries lightly with sifted powdered sugar, if desired.

YIELD: 18 rolls.

Continued on following page.

Breakfast and Breads

Continued from preceding page.

PRUNE FILLING: In a saucepan, combine 2 cups coarsely-snipped, pitted, dried prunes and enough water to come 1-inch above the prunes.
SIMMER, covered, 10 minutes; drain.
STIR in 1/2 cup chopped walnuts, 1/3 cup sugar, 2 teaspoons lemon juice and 1/2 teaspoon ground cinnamon.
COOL.

APRICOT FILLING: In a saucepan, combine 2 cups coarsely-snipped dried apricots and water to come 1-inch above the apricots.
SIMMER, covered, for 10 minutes; drain.
STIR in 1/3 cup sugar, 1 tablespoon butter or margarine and 1/2 teaspoon ground nutmeg.
COOL.

Macadamia Nut French Toast

4 lg. eggs, beaten
1/4 c. sugar
1/4 tsp. ground nutmeg
2/3 c. orange juice
1/3 c. milk
1 tsp. vanilla extract
1 (16 oz.) loaf Italian bread, cut into 1" slices

2/3 c. butter or margarine, melted
1/2 c. macadamia nuts, chopped
Garnishes: powdered sugar, ground nutmeg

COMBINE eggs and the next 5 ingredients, stirring well.
FIT bread slices in a single layer into a lightly-greased 13x9x2-inch baking dish. Pour egg mixture over bread slices; cover and refrigerate 8 hours, or overnight, turning bread once.
POUR butter into a 15x10x1-inch jellyroll pan; place bread slices in a single layer in pan.
BAKE at 400° for 10 minutes; sprinkle with nuts. Bake an additional 10 minutes. Garnish, if desired, and serve immediately with maple syrup.
YIELD: 6 servings.

Breakfast and Breads

Orange Marmalade Quick Bread

2 1/2 c. sifted flour	1 tsp. baking soda
1 tsp. salt	3/4 c. sugar
1 egg, beaten	1/2 c. thick orange marmalade
1/4 c. white vinegar	2 T. melted shortening
1 c. milk	

SIFT flour with baking soda, salt and sugar.
COMBINE egg and marmalade; stir in vinegar, milk and shortening.
POUR into a greased 9x5x3-inch loaf pan
BAKE for 1 hour.

THIS bread is really good toasted.

Overnight Coffee Cake

2/3 c. margarine	1 tsp. baking soda
1 c. sugar	2 T. powdered milk
1/2 c. brown sugar	1 tsp. salt
2 eggs, well beaten	1 tsp. cinnamon
2 c. flour, sifted	1 c. buttermilk
1 tsp. baking powder	

TOPPING:

3/4 c. brown sugar	1/4 tsp. nutmeg
1/4 tsp. cinnamon	3/4 c. chopped nuts, of choice

CREAM margarine, sugar and brown sugar.
ADD eggs and mix well.
MIX dry ingredients and add to creamed mixture alternately with the buttermilk.
POUR into greased baking dish or bundt pan (I like to use a bundt pan) and sprinkle with topping.
COVER and refrigerate overnight, or for several days, if you wish.
BAKE at 350° for 30 to 40 minutes.

Breakfast and Breads

Pear Relish

I like to use this relish with lamb. I never cooked lamb very often before, but lately I have been finding a large variety of ways to cook the lamb and find we really like it.

12 1/2 lb. pears, peeled & cored (I use Bosc pears)	6 med. onions, quartered
	1 T. salt
8 jalapeño peppers, seeded	1 T. celery seeds
6 red bell peppers, quartered	5 c. sugar
6 green bell peppers, quartered	5 c. white vinegar (5% acidity)

POSITION knife blade in food processor bowl; add pears, a few at a time.
PULSE 2 to 3 times, or until pears are chopped.
TRANSFER pears to a large Dutch oven.
REPEAT procedure until all pears, peppers and onions are chopped.
ADD salt and remaining ingredients to Dutch oven, stirring well.
BRING to a boil over medium heat; reduce heat and simmer 30 minutes, stirring occasionally.
SPOON hot relish into hot jars, filling to 1/2-inch from top.
REMOVE air bubbles; wipe jar rims.
COVER at once with metal lids, and screw on bands.
PROCESS in a boiling water bath 20 minutes.
YIELD; 14 pints.

Phyl's Zucchini Bread

3 eggs	2 tsp. baking powder
2 c. sugar	2 tsp. baking soda
1 c. vegetable oil	1 T. cinnamon
1 tsp. salt	1 T. vanilla
2 3/4 c. flour	1 c. chopped nuts
2 c. grated zucchini	

BEAT eggs; gradually add sugar to eggs. Add oil.
COMBINE dry ingredients and add to egg mixture alternately with zucchini.
STIR in nuts and vanilla.
PLACE in lightly-greased and floured loaf pans (2).
BAKE at 350° for 1 hour, using large pans. (You may use 3 smaller loaf pans, they should be baked at 350° for 50 minutes.)

Sopaipillas

This recipe was sent to me by a friend, Beverly Pareo, from Vequita, New Mexico. It is a Mexican bread that is also good for stuffed sopaipillas.

DISSOLVE 1 package yeast in 3/4 cup warm water; add 1 tablespoon oil.
COMBINE:

2 c. flour	1 tsp. salt
1 tsp. sugar	1/2 tsp. baking powder

COMBINE dry ingredients with yeast mixture; stir well.
KNEAD 15 to 20 times.
COVER with towel for 10 to 15 minutes.
ROLL about 1/4-inch thick; cut into squares or triangles.
FRY in hot oil about 1/2-inch deep; while frying, spoon oil over the top until they puff up.
THEN flip over; cook until golden. Drain.

YOU can stuff these with pinto bean or Spanish rice. Top with cheese and green chili sauce, or use as a bread with a Mexican meal.

Strawberry Bread

This bread adds a very festive touch to a holiday breakfast.

3 c. flour	2 c. sugar
1/2 c. nonfat dry milk	1 tsp. salt
1 tsp. baking soda	1 T. ground cinnamon

COMBINE the above ingredients; make a well in center and add 1 1/4 cups of vegetable oil.
STIR just until moist.
STIR IN:

1 (16 oz.) pkg. frozen, whole strawberries, chopped fine, or 2 heaping c. fresh berries	3 eggs, beaten 1/4 tsp. red food coloring 1 1/4 c. chopped pecans

GREASE 2 (8-inch) loaf pans; place waxed paper in bottom of pans and grease again.
SPOON batter into pans.
BAKE 1 hour at 350° or less.
LET stand overnight before slicing. (This bread can be very delicate. If you try to slice too soon, it may crumble.)

Streusel-Filled Coffee Cake

COFFEE CAKE:

1 1/2 c. flour	1/4 c. shortening
3 tsp. baking powder	1 egg
1/2 tsp. salt	1 tsp. vanilla
3/4 c. sugar	1/2 c. milk

FILLING & TOPPING:	2 tsp. cinnamon
1/2 c. brown sugar	2 T. butter, melted
2 T. flour	1/2 c. nuts, chopped

MIX sugar, flour and cinnamon together; blend in melted butter.
STIR in nuts; mix well and use as filling and topping. Set aside.
MIX together flour, baking powder, salt and sugar; cut in shortening until mixture is like fine cornmeal.
BLEND in well-beaten egg; mix with milk. Blend in vanilla and beat just enough to mix well.
POUR half of batter into greased and floured 6x10-inch pan.
SPRINKLE half of streusel mixture on top of batter.
ADD remaining batter and sprinkle remaining streusel mixture over top.
BAKE at 375° for 25 to 30 minutes.

THIS coffee cake is good also when you replace the milk with 1 cup sour cream.

Sweet Potato Spoon Bread

3 lg. sweet potatoes	1 1/2 tsp. cinnamon
1/4 c. yellow cornmeal	1 tsp. salt
2 c. milk	1/2 c. all-purpose flour
4 T. unsalted butter	1/4 c. honey
1/4 c. light brown sugar	4 lg. eggs
1/4 tsp. ground nutmeg	1 c. heavy cream
1/4 tsp. ground cloves	

HEAT oven to 400°.
BAKE sweet potatoes until soft when pierced with a fork, 40 to 45 minutes.
LET cool; peel and discard skins.
REDUCE heat to 350°.
IN medium saucepan over medium heat, combine cornmeal, milk, butter, brown sugar, spices, salt, and 1 cup water.
COOK, stirring, until slightly thickened, about 10 minutes.
LET COOL.
BUTTER a 2-quart baking dish.
PLACE cornmeal mixture, sweet potatoes, flour, honey, eggs and cream in a food processor.
PROCESS until smooth; pour into dish.
BAKE until golden brown, about 45 minutes.
SERVE.
YIELD: 8 to 10 servings.

Waffles

2 c. flour, sifted	2 eggs, separated
3 tsp. baking powder	1 2/3 c. milk
2 T. sugar	1/2 c. shortening, softened
3/4 tsp. salt	Fruit batter (recipe below)

PREHEAT waffle iron; make sure all ingredients are room temperature.
SIFT flour, baking powder, sugar and salt together; set aside.
CREAM egg yolks and shortening together; add milk and beat well.
COMBINE dry ingredients and milk mixture; stir until smooth.
BEAT egg whites until stiff; fold into batter.
POUR batter into waffle iron, following directions per size of iron.
COOK until iron stops steaming; do not open iron before the steam stops.

FRUIT BUTTER:

10 oz. frozen fruit, such as strawberries, peaches, blueberries, etc., or 1 c. fresh fruit	1/2 lb. butter, softened 1 c. powdered sugar

PLACE ingredients in blender or food processor until completely smooth.

Walnut Bread

3 c. sifted all-purpose flour	1 egg, beaten
1 c. sugar	1/4 c. soft shortening
4 tsp. baking powder	1 1/2 c. milk
1 1/2 tsp. salt	1 tsp. vanilla
1 1/2 c. coarsely-chopped walnuts, divided	

RESIFT flour with sugar, baking powder and salt into mixing bowl.
STIR in 1 1/4 cups of the walnuts.
ADD egg, shortening, milk and vanilla.
MIX just until ingredients are blended.
TURN into greased and floured loaf pan, 9x5x3 inches.
SPRINKLE remaining 1/4 cup walnuts over the top.
BAKE at 350° for 60 to 70 minutes.
LET loaf stand in pan 10 minutes, then turn out onto wire rack to cool.
YIELD: 1 large loaf.

Breakfast and Breads

Zucchini Bread

3 eggs
2 c. sugar
3/4 c. vegetable oil
2 c. all-purpose flour
1/2 tsp. baking powder
2 tsp. baking soda
1 tsp. salt

3 tsp. ground cinnamon
2 c. peeled, grated & well-
    drained zucchini
1 T. vanilla extract
1 c. chopped nuts, or 1/2 c.
    each nuts & raisins

GREASE 2 (9x5x3-inch) loaf pans and preheat oven to 350°.
BLEND eggs, sugar and oil in a large mixing bowl.
STIR in flour, baking powder, baking soda, salt and cinnamon. Mix well.
STIR in zucchini, vanilla and nuts.
DIVIDE batter evenly between prepared pans. and bake 45 minutes, or until a cake tester inserted in center of loaf comes out clean (toothpick).
YIELD: 2 loaves.

Notes &
Recipes

Breakfast and Breads

SALADS

List Your Favorite Recipes

Recipes   **Page**

_____   _____

_____   _____

_____   _____

_____   _____

_____   _____

_____   _____

_____   _____

_____   _____

_____   _____

_____   _____

_____   _____

_____   _____

_____   _____

_____   _____

_____   _____

_____   _____

_____   _____

Ambrosia Salad

9 oranges, peeled, seeded &
   sectioned
2 (20 oz.) cans crushed
   pineapple, drained

1 c. honey
1 to 2 tsp. almond extract
1 c. flaked coconut

COMBINE all ingredients. Cover mixture and chill at least 8 hours
before serving.
YIELD: 6 to 8 servings.

Apple-Cream Cheese Salad

1 c. hot water
2/3 c. (6 oz.) sm. red
   cinnamon candies
1 (3 oz.) pkg. lemon gelatin
1 1/2 c. sweetened applesauce

1 (8 oz.) pkg. cream cheese,
   softened
1/2 c. chopped nuts of choice
1/2 c. finely-chopped celery
1/2 c. mayonnaise

POUR hot water over cinnamon candies to dissolve. Add gelatin. Stir
until completely dissolved. Add applesauce.
POUR half of mixture in an 8x8x2-inch pan; chill.
BLEND together cream cheese, nuts and celery. Add mayonnaise and
spread in a layer over firm apple mixture.
POUR on remaining apple mixture. Chill until firm and unmold.
GARNISH with small bunches of sugared grapes.
YIELD: 6 servings.

Buffet Fresh Green Salad

2/3 c. olive oil or salad oil
1/3 c. lemon juice
2 tsp. sugar
1/2 tsp. dried mint, crushed
(opt.)
1/8 tsp. freshly-ground black
pepper
1/4 tsp. salt

2 c. torn spinach leaves
2 c. lettuce or radish leaves*
1 bunch (2 c.) watercress*
2 c. parsley sprigs*
1 1/2 c. Feta cheese, crumbled
1 cucumber, seeded & coarsely
shredded

DRESSING: In a screw-top jar, combine the first 6 ingredients.
COVER; shake well.
SERVE the dressing, greens, cheese and cucumber separately.
LET guests assemble their own salads.
STIR dressing frequently during serving.
YIELD: 6 to 8 servings.

*ANY of these greens may be substituted by greens of your choice.

Carrot-Orange Salad

This is a very, very easy salad, but also very colorful and tasty.

2 c. (4 med.) grated carrots
1 c. (2 med.) orange sections

3 T. sugar
1/4 c. sour cream

COMBINE all ingredients; mix well and chill.
YIELD: 4 servings.

Cauliflower Salad

1 c. bacon bits (bottled or
fresh)
1 sm. head cauliflower
1 (10 oz.) pkg. frozen peas
1/4 to 1/2 c. sliced onions

1 c. diced Cheddar cheese
1 to 2 c. mayonnaise
1 T. seasoned salt, or if available,
Salad Supreme
1/4 tsp. garlic powder

MIX all ingredients and refrigerate overnight before serving.

Cheddar Cheese and Apple Salad

2 lg. red apples, cored & diced   1/4 c. sour cream
1 c. thinly-sliced celery   1 tsp. tarragon vinegar
3/4 c. pineapple tidbits, drained 1 T. prepared horseradish
1/2 c. Cheddar cheese, diced   Salad greens
1/4 c. mayonnaise

MIX the first 4 ingredients in a bowl.
MIX remaining ingredients; combine all ingredients and toss well.
SERVE over salad greens.
YIELD: 4 to 6 servings.

Chilled Corn Salad

1 (12 oz.) can whole kernel   2 T. cider vinegar
   corn, drained   1 T. vegetable oil
1 sm. onion, chopped   1/4 tsp. salt
1/2 c. chopped green pepper   1/4 tsp. pepper
2 T. minced fresh parsley   Garnish, if desired

COMBINE all ingredients; cover and chill at least 4 hours before serving.
YIELD: 4 to 6 servings.

Christmas Salad

1 (3 oz.) pkg. lime gelatin
3/4 c. mini marshmallows
1 c. pineapple juice
1 (3 oz.) pkg. cream cheese
1/4 c. finely-chopped pecans
2 c. freshly-whipped light cream
(whipped with 3 T. sugar)
1 c. mayonnaise
1 (6 oz.) pkg. red gelatin
1 sm. can jellied cranberries

DISSOLVE lime gelatin into 1 cup boiling water.
STIR marshmallows into warm gelatin.
MIX pineapple juice, chopped pecans and cream cheese together until well blended; mix in whipped cream (may use Cool Whip) and mayonnaise.
ADD cream cheese mixture to lime gelatin mixture; pour into a 9x13-inch pan.
COOL and refrigerate until firm.
MIX red gelatin with 1 1/2 cups boiling water. Add jellied cranberries; mix well.
POUR over top of lime gelatin mixture; refrigerate until firm.
GARNISH as desired.
YIELD: 10 to 12 servings.

Cookie Salad

2 c. buttermilk
1 lg. pkg. instant vanilla
pudding
1 (16 oz.) ctn. Cool Whip
(I prefer to whip fresh
whipping cream)
2 cans mandarin oranges, drained
18 striped chocolate cookies

CRUSH cookies; set aside.
MIX milk and pudding. Add drained oranges.
FOLD in whipped cream or Cool Whip and cookies. (Save some of the crushed cookies for the top of the salad.)

Cranberry Fluff

2 c. raw cranberries, finely chopped	1/2 c. walnuts, chopped
3 c. mini marshmallows	1/4 tsp. salt
3/4 c. sugar	4 oz. Cool Whip (half of a sm. ctn.), or fresh whipped half &
2 c. diced, unpeeled tart apples	half with 2 T. sugar
1/2 c. seedless grapes	1/4 c. mayonnaise

COMBINE cranberries, marshmallows, apples, grapes, nuts and salt.
COVER and set in refrigerator overnight.
FOLD in the mayonnaise and then the whipped cream or Cool Whip.
YIELD: 8 to 10 servings.

Cranberry-Orange Mold

1 1/2 c. boiling water	1 c. (16 oz.) whole-berry cranberry sauce
1 (8-serving-size) or 2 (4-serving-size) pkg. gelatin cranberry gelatin	1 c. cold water
1/2 tsp. ground cinnamon	1 orange, sectioned & diced
	1/2 c. chopped walnuts

STIR boiling water into gelatin and cinnamon in large bowl at least 2 minutes until completely dissolved.
STIR in cranberry sauce until melted; stir in cold water.
REFRIGERATE about 1 1/2 hours or until thickened (spoon drawn through leaves definite impression).
STIR in orange and walnuts.
SPOON into 5-cup mold.
REFRIGERATE 4 hours or until firm.
UNMOLD.
GARNISH as desired.
YIELD: 10 servings.

TO UNMOLD:
DIP mold in warm water for about 15 seconds.
GENTLY pull gelatin from around edges with moist fingers.
PLACE moistened serving plate on top of mold.
INVERT mold and plate. Holding mold and plate together, shake slightly to loosen.
GENTLY remove mold; center gelatin on plate.

Cranberry-Raspberry Sherbet Mold

2 (3 oz.) pkg. raspberry
    gelatin
1 1/2 c. boiling water
1 pt. raspberry sherbet
1 T. lemon juice

1 (16 oz.) can whole-berry
    cranberry sauce
Lettuce leaves for garnish, may
    use any greens you wish

DISSOLVE raspberry gelatin in boiling water. Stir in sherbet and lemon juice; chill.

MASH cranberry sauce slightly with fork; fold in gelatin mixture.

TURN mixture into 5-cup ring mold (you may wish to spray your mold with a vegetable spray, makes it much easier to unmold).

CHILL until firm.

UNMOLD onto garnish of your choice.

YIELD: 8 to 10 servings.

Creamy Spinach Salad

8 slices bacon
1/2 c. mayonnaise
2 T. milk, half & half, or
    light cream
1 T. honey
1 T. lemon juice

Salt & pepper
6 c. fresh spinach, rinsed, stems
    removed & torn
1 c. sliced fresh mushrooms
1 med. tomato, chopped
2 hard-cooked eggs, chopped

COOK the bacon until it's crisp; drain the slices on paper toweling. Crumble 4 of the bacon slices.

RESERVE the remaining 4 slices and 1 teaspoon to 1 tablespoon of the drippings; discard the remaining drippings.

IN a bowl, combine mayonnaise, milk, honey, lemon, salt, pepper, bacon, and as much of the bacon drippings as you like.

STIR until well combined.

IN a salad bowl, lightly toss the spinach, mushrooms, tomatoes and eggs.

POUR the dressing over the spinach; toss spinach to coat.

GARNISH each serving with a slice of bacon.

YIELD: 4 servings.

Salads

Crunchy Pea Salad

1 (10 oz.) pkg. sm. frozen peas
1 c. celery, diced
1 c. cauliflower, diced
1/4 c. green onion, diced
2 T. pimento
1 c. roasted cashews
1/4 c. bacon, cooked &
   crumbled

1/4 c. sour cream
3/4 c. prepared Hidden Valley
   salad dressing (original)
1/2 tsp. Dijon mustard
1/4 tsp. garlic salt
1/8 tsp. white pepper

RINSE peas in hot water; drain.
COMBINE vegetables and sour cream.
MIX together prepared dressing, mustard and garlic; pour over salad.
TOSS gently and chill.
ADD nuts and bacon just before serving.

Frozen Cherry Salad Loaf

1 (16 oz.) can dark sweet
   cherries, drained
1 (8 3/4 oz.) can crushed
   pineapple, drained
1 (11 oz.) can mandarin
   oranges, drained

1 (8 oz.) pkg. cream cheese
1 c. sour cream, softened
1/4 c. sugar
1/4 tsp. salt
2 c. mini marshmallows
1/2 c. chopped pecans (opt.)

RESERVE a few cherries and orange segments for garnish.
BEAT cream cheese until fluffy, and blend in sour cream, sugar and salt.
FOLD in fruits, marshmallows and pecans.
POUR into a 4 1/2 x 8 1/2-inch loaf pan (spray pan with vegetable cooking spray to allow for easy unmolding).
FREEZE for 6 hours or overnight.
UNMOLD and garnish with reserved fruit in a flower design.
YIELD: 8 to 10 servings.

Salads   53

Frozen Cranberry Salad

1 1/2 c. crushed pineapple, drained
1 c. jellied cranberries
1 c. sour cream
1 T. lemon juice
1 c. mini marshmallows
1 sliced banana
1/2 c. chopped nuts of choice
1/8 tsp. salt

MIX all ingredients together. Place in a flat pan.
FREEZE until firm; cut to desired size servings.
PLACE on serving plate. Top with fresh whipped cream.
YIELD: 10 to 12 servings.

Fruit Mold with Ginger

1 (3 oz.) pkg. apricot-flavored gelatin
2 c. boiling water
1/3 c. coarsely-cut dates (opt.)
2 med. unpeeled apples, cored & diced
2 med. unpeeled pears, cored & diced
1/3 c. chopped walnuts
Lettuce leaves (opt.)
Ginger Dressing

DISSOLVE gelatin in boiling water; stir in dates. Chill until consistency of unbeaten egg whites.
FOLD in pears, apples and walnuts.
POUR into lightly-oiled 4-cup mold; cover and chill until firm.
UNMOLD on lettuce leaves, if desired.

GINGER DRESSING:
1/3 c. mayonnaise
1/3 c. sour cream
2 T. crystallized ginger

COMBINE all ingredients, stirring well; chill.
YIELD: 2/3 cup.

54   *Salads*

Grandma Velma's Cranberry Salad

There was never a holiday without Grandma Velma's cranberry salad, and we still never let one go by without it, and our fond and loving memories of Grandma.

1/2 lb. cranberries, ground	1/2 c. chopped nuts of choice
1 c. sugar	3 bananas, sliced
1 lb. Tokay grapes, sliced in half	1/2 pt. (1 c.) whipping cream

GRIND cranberries. Add 1 cup of sugar; let stand overnight in refrigerator. WHEN ready to serve, add sliced grapes, chopped nuts, sliced bananas, and whipping cream (which you have whipped just previously to assembling salad).
GENTLY stir all ingredients together and serve.
GARNISH as desired.

Green Bean, Walnut Salad with Feta Cheese

1 c. coarsely-chopped walnuts	1/4 tsp. pepper
3/4 c. olive oil	1 1/2 lb. fresh green beans; or
1/4 c. white vinegar	frozen, thawed & dried; or
1 T. chopped fresh dill	canned, drained & dried
(or 1 tsp. dried dill)	1 sm. purple onion, thinly sliced
1/2 tsp. minced garlic	1 (4 oz.) pkg. crumbled Feta
1/4 tsp. salt	cheese

BAKE walnuts in a shallow pan at 350°, stirring occasionally, 5 to 10 minutes or until toasted; set aside.
COMBINE oil and the next 5 ingredients; cover and chill.
CUT green beans into thirds and arrange in steamer basket over boiling water (if using fresh beans). Cover and steam 15 minutes or until green beans are crisp-tender.
IMMEDIATELY plunge green beans into cold water to stop cooking process; drain and pat dry.
COMBINE walnuts, beans, onion and cheese in a large bowl; toss well.
COVER and chill.
POUR oil mixture over bean mixture 1 hour before serving; toss just before serving.
YIELD: 6 servings.

Salads   55

Heavenly Food

This recipe is from Evelyn Rupple from Medina, Wisconsin. Evelyn has many talents, she is a retired teacher, artist, and a great cook.

1 c. sugar	4 oranges, peeled & sliced
1/2 lb. chopped dates	4 bananas, sliced
4 T. flour	4 apples, unpeeled & chopped
1 tsp. baking powder	1/2 pt. whipping cream, whipped
2 eggs	(you may use Cool Whip)
1/2 lb. nutmeats	

MIX cake together; pour into a greased 8x8-inch pan.
BAKE at 300° for 1/2 hour.
WHEN cake is cooled, crumble cake into bite-size pieces.
IN a large glass serving bowl, place a layer of crumbled cake on the bottom.
COVER this layer with slices of oranges, bananas and chopped, unpeeled apples.
COVER the fruit with whipped cream, then make another layer of cake, then fruit, then whipped cream.
MAKE as many layers as you can, ending with the whipped cream.
THIS can be served as a dessert or fruit salad.

Orange Jello Salad

1 (6 oz.) pkg. orange gelatin	1/2 c. crushed pineapple, drained
1 c. hot water	1/2 c. coconut
3 c. cold water	1/2 c. chopped pecans
2 c. grated carrots	

DISSOLVE gelatin in hot water, then add cold water; mix well.
REFRIGERATE until mixture starts to congeal.
ADD remaining ingredients.
REFRIGERATE until firm.

Oriental Cabbage Salad

1 head cabbage, chopped fine
6 to 7 green onions with tops,
    chopped
1/2 c. butter
2 pkg. Ramen noodles,
    crushed (chicken flavor)

1/2 c. sesame seeds or sunflower
    seeds
1 (3 oz.) pkg. slivered almonds
1 c. oil
1 c. sugar
2 T. soy sauce
1/2 c. vinegar

BROWN noodles in butter.
ADD sesame or sunflower seeds and almonds.
CONTINUE to brown; add to cabbage and onions.
MIX oil, soy sauce and vinegar together; top above mixture.
MAKE this salad one day ahead of use.
YIELD: 8 to 10 servings.

Original Waldorf Salad

2 T. orange juice
3 lg. tart red apples, unpeeled
    & diced
1/2 c. diced celery
1/2 c. sour cream

1/2 c. raisins
1/4 c. chopped pecans or walnuts
1 1/2 tsp. sugar
Lettuce leaves (opt.)

SPRINKLE orange juice over apples; toss gently and drain.
COMBINE apples, celery and the next 4 ingredients; stir well.
COVER and chill.
SERVE on lettuce leaves, if desired.
YIELD: 6 servings.

Pretzel Jello Salad

2 1/2 c. pretzels, coarsely
    crushed
3 T. sugar
1/2 c. margarine
1 (8 oz.) pkg. cream cheese
1 c. sugar

1 lg. ctn. Cool Whip
2 (3 oz.) pkg. strawberry gelatin
    or 1 (6 oz.) size
2 c. boiling water
2 (10 oz.) pkg. frozen
    strawberries

MIX pretzels, margarine and sugar.
BAKE in a 9x13-inch pan at 350° for 10 minutes; cool completely.
CREAM cheese and blend in 1 cup sugar.
ADD Cool Whip, mixing well; spread over cooled pretzels.
DISSOLVE gelatin in boiling water; add frozen strawberries, breaking up with a fork as you stir.
CHILL until slightly thickened; pour over Cool Whip layer and chill until set.
GARNISH as desired.
YIELD: 8 to 10 servings.

Pea Salad

2 cans peas, drained
4 hard-boiled eggs, peeled
    & diced
2 T. sweet pickles, diced
Pinch of sugar

1 sm. onion, diced
1 c. celery, diced
1/2 c. Hellmann's mayonnaise,
    or enough to cover
Salt & pepper, to taste

MIX all ingredients together and refrigerate until serving.

Pickled Beets

1 c. sugar	3 T. cooking oil
2 level T. cornstarch	1 tsp. vanilla
1 c. vinegar	Dash of salt
24 cloves	3 (No. 303) cans beets
3 T. catsup	1 1/2 c. beet juice

MIX sugar and cornstarch in saucepan; add vinegar, cloves, catsup, oil, vanilla and salt; mix well. Cut beets into bite-size pieces.
ADD beets and beet juice to mixture.
COOK over medium heat about 3 minutes or until thick. Store in refrigerator.
SERVE cold.

Ribbon Salad

2 (3 oz.) pkg. lime gelatin	1 (8 oz.) pkg. cream cheese
1 (3 oz.) pkg. lemon gelatin	1 (20 oz.) can crushed pineapple
2 (3 oz.) pkg. cherry gelatin	1 c. mayonnaise
1/2 c. mini marshmallows	1 c. whipping cream

IN a 9x13-inch glass casserole dish, mix cherry gelatin with 2 cups hot water and 2 cups cold water; chill until firm.
IN the top of a double boiler, mix lemon gelatin with 1 cup hot water and drained juice from the pineapple; add marshmallows and heat until melted.
REMOVE from heat and add cream cheese; beat until smooth.
COOL slightly, then add crushed pineapple and mayonnaise.
FOLD in whipped cream and chill until thick.
POUR over cherry gelatin and sprinkle with chopped nuts.
MIX lime gelatin with 2 cups hot water and 2 cups cold water; chill until thick and pour over lemon gelatin layer.
CHILL for 24 hours.
YIELD: 24 servings.

Santa Salad

1 (6 oz.) pkg. cherry gelatin
1 c. hot water
1 (13 1/2 oz.) can pineapple
    chunks or tidbits

1 qt. (32 oz.) frozen strawberries,
    thawed
1 pt. (16 oz.) sour cream
1 (9") round cake pan

DISSOLVE gelatin in hot water. Add pineapple, strawberries and juice from both fruits; stir well.
POUR half the mixture into a 9-inch round cake pan; chill until firm.
SPREAD sour cream evenly over the top; add the remaining gelatin mixture and chill until firm.
SERVE from pan, or you could unmold and garnish as desired.
YIELD: 6 to 8 servings.

Seafoam Salad

1 lg. can pears, mashed
1 (3 oz.) pkg. lime gelatin
1 (8 oz.) pkg. cream cheese

2 T. cream
1 c. heavy cream, whipped
    (half & half is fine)

DRAIN juice from pears (reserve 1 cup of pear juice).
HEAT the 1 cup of reserved pear juice to boiling; pour over gelatin and stir until dissolved; cool.
BEAT cream cheese and 2 tablespoon cream until smooth; add gelatin mixture and beat until partly thickened.
FOLD in well-drained mashed pears, along with whipped cream.
POUR into mold or square pan; chill until firm.
SERVE unmolded; or if you used square pan, cut into squares, place on crisp lettuce and garnish with a red cherry.

Salads

Spinach Salad

2 lb. fresh spinach, chopped
10 hard-boiled eggs, sliced
  crosswise
1 lb. bacon, fried & crumbled

1 sm. head lettuce, shredded
1 c. sliced green onions
1 1/2 c. frozen green peas,
  uncooked

PLACE in order given in a 10x14-inch glass pan or a very large salad bowl.
BLEND together:

2 1/2 c. mayonnaise
2 1/2 c. sour cream

1 tsp. Worcestershire sauce
1 tsp. lemon juice

SPREAD over salad.
TOP with 1/2 cup grated Swiss cheese.
COVER with foil and chill 12 hours.
DO not toss.
YIELD: 14 to 16 servings.

Vegetable Salad

1 can French-style green
  beans, drained
1 can peas, drained
1 (7 oz.) jar pimento, drained
1 c. onion, diced
1 c. green pepper, chopped

1 c. celery, diced
1 c. sugar
3/4 c. vinegar
1/2 c. salad oil
1 tsp. salt

MIX sugar, vinegar, salad oil and salt until sugar dissolves.
MIX with vegetables.
MAKE one day before serving.
KEEP refrigerated (will keep several weeks).

Salads   **61**

Vegetable Salad

1 c. sugar	1 can French-style green beans
1/2 c. salad oil	1 can green peas
1/2 tsp. pepper	1/2 c. onion, chopped
1/2 tsp. dill seed	1 sm. jar mushrooms
3/4 c. vinegar	1/4 c. chopped green pepper
1 tsp. salt	1 sm. jar diced pimento
1 T. water	1 1/2 c. raw bits of cauliflower
1 can whole kernel white corn	

DRESSING: Mix sugar, oil, pepper, dill seed, vinegar, salt and water, stirring until sugar is dissolved.
DRAIN canned vegetables thoroughly; mix together all ingredients and let stand overnight in refrigerator.
YIELD: 12 servings.

Wild Rice with Cranberries and Caramelized Onions

2 c. chicken broth	3 med. onions, sliced into thin
1/2 c. brown sugar	wedges
1/2 c. wild rice	2 tsp. brown sugar
3 T. butter or margarine	1 c. craisins (sweetened dried
1/2 tsp. finely-grated orange zest	cranberries)

COMBINE chicken broth and both rices in a medium saucepan.
BRING to a boil over medium-high heat.
REDUCE heat to low.
COVER and simmer 45 minutes, or until rice is tender and the liquid is absorbed.
MEANWHILE, melt butter in a medium skillet over medium-high heat.
ADD onions and brown sugar.
COOK 6 minutes, or until liquid is absorbed and onions are soft and translucent.
REDUCE heat to low. Slowly cook onions, stirring often, for 25 minutes or until they are caramel color.
STIR in dried cranberries.
COVER and cook over low heat for 10 minutes, or until cranberries swell.
GENTLY fold cranberry mixture and orange zest into cooked rice.
YIELD: 4 to 6 servings.

Yogurt Waldorf Salad

1 Red Delicious apple, unpeeled & chopped	1 stalk celery, sliced diagonally
1 Granny Smith apple, unpeeled & chopped	1 (8 oz.) ctn. plain yogurt
	1 T. honey
1 pear, unpeeled & chopped	1 tsp. grated orange rind
1 T. lemon juice	1/4 c. slivered almonds, toasted
1/4 c. golden raisins	Celery leaves, for garnish

COMBINE the first 3 ingredients in a medium-size bowl. Sprinkle lemon juice over fruit mixture and toss gently.

STIR in golden raisins and celery; set aside.

COMBINE yogurt, honey and orange rind, stirring well.

STIR 1/4 cup yogurt mixture into fruit mixture.

SPOON salad into serving bowl and sprinkle with almonds. Garnish, if desired.

SERVE with remaining dressing.

YIELD: 6 servings.

Notes &
Recipes

SOUPS

List Your Favorite Recipes

Recipes   **Page**

_____   _____

_____   _____

_____   _____

_____   _____

_____   _____

_____   _____

_____   _____

_____   _____

_____   _____

_____   _____

_____   _____

_____   _____

_____   _____

_____   _____

_____   _____

_____   _____

Acorn Squash Soup

4 acorn squash
3 carrots, sliced
1 onion, sliced
1/3 c. water
2 T. butter
1 T. all-purpose flour
1 tsp. salt
1/2 to 1 tsp. pepper
2 (14 1/2 oz.) cans chicken
  broth

1/2 c. sherry
1/2 tsp. ground nutmeg
1/8 tsp. paprika
Dash of ground allspice
Dash of red pepper
1 c. half & half
1 1/2 T. sherry (opt.)
Kale leaves (opt.)
Paprika

CUT squash in half lengthwise and remove seeds.
PLACE squash, cut-side down, in a broiler pan.
ADD hot water to pan to a depth of 1-inch.
BAKE at 350° for 30 minutes.
SPOON pulp from squash to create a serving bowl, reserving pulp.
PLACE carrots and onion in a saucepan; cover with water.
BRING to a boil; cover, reduce heat and simmer 15 minutes or until vegetables are tender.
DRAIN; combine vegetables with reserved pulp and 1/3 cup water in container of an electric blender or food processor.
PROCESS 30 seconds or until mixture is smooth. Set aside.
MELT butter in a large Dutch oven over low heat. Add flour, salt and pepper, stirring until smooth.
COOK 1 minute, stirring constantly.
GRADUALLY add puréed vegetable mixture, chicken broth and the next 5 ingredients; bring to a boil.
COVER, reduce heat and simmer 1 hour, stirring occasionally.
STIR in half & half and, if desired, 1 1/2 tablespoons sherry.
COOK until heated.
IF desired, serve in squash shells on a bed of kale.
SPRINKLE with paprika.
YIELD: 8 servings.

Beef Soup

1 1/2 lb. soup meat	1 tsp. salt
1/2 tsp. pepper	2 bay leaves
4 to 5 med. carrots, sliced	1/2 c. onion, chopped
1 c. celery, chopped	1 c. cabbage, chopped
1 can Italian-style tomatoes	1 T. Worcestershire sauce
(may use stewed tomatoes)	Pinch of basil or any other spice
1 beef bouillon cube	of choice

COVER meat with cold water in a heavy kettle. Add salt, pepper and bay leaves.
LET it come to bubbly stage while preparing vegetables.
TURN heat to low and add celery, onions, carrots, cabbage and basil; simmer at least 2 1/2 hours, or until meat is very tender.
REMOVE meat and bay leaves; cut meat into bite-size pieces.
ADD meat back to liquid, along with tomatoes, Worcestershire sauce and bouillon cube; simmer for 1/2 hour longer and serve.
YIELD: 6 servings.

Chicken Gumbo

1 (3 to 3 1/2 lb.) chicken, cut in pieces	6 lg. tomatoes, peeled & chopped
1/2 lb. ham, cut in 1/2" cubes	2 c. sliced okra or cabbage
1/4 c. salad oil	1 qt. boiling water
1 c. chopped onion	1 bay leaf
1/3 c. chopped green pepper	2 tsp. salt
2 T. chopped jalapeño pepper	1/2 tsp. pepper
	Cooked rice, about 4 c.

COOK rice according to package directions; set aside.
COOK chicken pieces and ham in salad oil in large Dutch oven until browned.
ADD remaining ingredients, except rice; simmer until tender, about 45 minutes.
TO serve, place spoonfuls of cooked rice (about 1/2 cup) in soup bowls or plates.
LADLE gumbo over rice.
YIELD: 8 servings.

Christmas Eve Chili

2 lg. onions, chopped	2 tsp. dried whole oregano
1 stalk celery, chopped	1/2 tsp. cumin seeds
3 cloves garlic, minced	1 (28 oz.) can whole tomatoes,
1 jalapeño pepper, finely	undrained & chopped
chopped	1 (6 oz.) can tomato paste
1 T. vegetable oil	1/4 c. chili powder
3 lb. boneless chuck roast,	1/2 tsp. salt
diced	3 1/2 c. water

SAUTÉ onion, celery, garlic and jalapeño pepper in hot oil until tender; set aside.

COMBINE meat, oregano and cumin in a Dutch oven; cook until meat is browned; drain well.

ADD onion mixture, tomatoes, tomato paste, chili powder, salt and water to meat mixture.

BRING to a boil. Reduce heat and simmer, uncovered, 1 1/2 to 2 hours, stirring occasionally.

YIELD: 5 cups.

Clam Chowder

1 can minced clams	7 to 10 drops Tabasco sauce
1 onion, chopped	2 dashes Worcestershire sauce
3 or 4 potatoes, chopped	1/2 tsp. garlic salt
3 or 4 celery stalks, chopped	1/4 tsp. paprika
2 cans cream of mushroom	1 tsp. basil
soup	Milk

SAUTÉ onion, celery and potatoes in oil for 10 minutes. Add 1 to 2 inches of water. Continue adding water until the potatoes are nearly done.

ADD the mushroom soup and clams with the juice; add all the spices. Simmer.

EIGHT minutes before serving, pour in as much milk as you desire.

Creamy Fish Soup

2 lb. fish fillets (haddock or	2 lemon slices
cod, fresh or frozen)	1 T. salt
1 qt. water	1/4 tsp. pepper
5 parsley sprigs	1 c. light cream
2 sm. carrots, peeled	2 egg yolks
3 branches celery	3 T. chopped parsley, dill or
2 med. onions, peeled	chives

COMBINE fish, water, parsley sprigs, carrots, celery, onions, lemon, salt and pepper in kettle; simmer 1 to 2 hours.
STRAIN.
BEAT cream and egg yolks in large bowl; add chopped parsley.
POUR hot stock over cream-egg mixture; blend thoroughly and serve at once.
YIELD: 4 to 6 servings.

Curried Cauliflower Soup

1 1/2 tsp. curry powder	1 stalk celery, diced
1 T. butter	1/2 c. half & half
3 1/2 c. turkey broth	Worcestershire sauce, to taste
1 lg. head cauliflower, cut	Salt, to taste
into flowerets	Freshly-grated nutmeg, to taste
1 sm. onion, minced	2 T. chopped parsley

COOK curry powder in butter in heavy 4-quart saucepan for a few minutes, stirring constantly, to release its flavor.
ADD broth, cauliflower, onion and celery.
COOK, covered, for 20 minutes or until cauliflower is very tender.
PURÉE, a portion at a time, in blender or food processor until very smooth.
POUR purée into saucepan. Add half & half, mixing well. Heat thoroughly.
SEASON to taste with Worcestershire sauce, salt and nutmeg.
LADLE soup into individual bowls and garnish with parsley.
YIELD: 6 cups.

Soups

French Onion Soup

4 lg. onions, thinly sliced & separated into rings	1/4 c. dry white wine
1/2 c. butter or margarine, melted	1/8 to 1/4 tsp. pepper
1 (10 3/4 oz.) can beef broth, undiluted	8 (3/4" thick) slices French bread, toasted
2 c. water	8 slices Mozzarella cheese
	1/2 c. grated Parmesan cheese

SAUTÉ onion in butter in a Dutch oven until tender; blend in flour, stirring until smooth.
GRADUALLY add chicken broth, beef broth, water and wine.
BRING to a boil; reduce heat and simmer 15 minutes. Add pepper.
PLACE 8 ovenproof serving bowls on a baking sheet.
PLACE 1 bread slice in each bowl; ladle soup over bread.
TOP with 1 cheese slice. Sprinkle with Parmesan cheese.
BROIL 6 inches from heat until cheese melts.
YIELD: 8 cups.

Green Bean Soup

1 ham bone with meat	1 sm. onion, minced
2 tsp. salt	1 1/2 c. diced, peeled potatoes
1 tsp. pepper	2 c. cut green beans
1 tsp. garlic salt	1/2 to 1 c. light cream
8 to 10 sprigs parsley	1 T. butter or margarine

PLACE ham bone in soup kettle with water to cover; bring to a boil, lower heat and simmer 2 hours, adding more water if needed.
ADD onion, potatoes, beans and spices. Cook until vegetables are tender, 20 to 30 minutes.
JUST before serving, blend in cream and butter.
YIELD: 8 to 10 servings.

Macaroni and Cheese Soup

1 c. elbow macaroni, uncooked
1/4 c. butter or margarine
1/2 c. finely-chopped carrots
1/2 c. finely-chopped celery
1 sm. onion, finely chopped
4 c. milk
2 T. water
1/2 c. frozen peas
1 1/2 c. (6 oz.) shredded process American cheese
2 T. chicken-flavored bouillon granules
1/2 tsp. ground white pepper
2 T. cornstarch
1 (8 oz.) can whole kernel corn, drained

COOK macaroni according to package directions, omitting salt; drain. Rinse with cold water; drain and set aside.

MELT butter in a large skillet over medium-high heat. Add carrot, celery and onion. Cook, stirring constantly, 5 to 7 minutes or until tender. Remove vegetable mixture from heat; set aside.

COMBINE milk and cheese in a heavy Dutch oven and cook over medium heat, stirring often, until cheese melts. Stir in bouillon granules and pepper.

COMBINE cornstarch and water, stirring well; stir into milk mixture. Cook over medium heat, stirring constantly, until mixture thickens and comes to a boil. Boil 1 minute, stirring constantly.

STIR in macaroni, vegetable mixture, corn and peas; cook over low heat, stirring constantly, until thoroughly heated.

YIELD: 8 cups.

Minestrone-Turkey Soup

1 meaty turkey carcass, cut
   apart
1 T. instant chicken bouillon
   granules
1 bay leaf
2 c. shredded cabbage
1 (14 1/2 oz.) can stewed
   tomatoes, cut up

1 (15 oz.) can Great Northern
   beans, drained
1 (15 oz.) can garbanzo beans,
   drained
1 lg. onion, chopped
1 clove garlic, minced
1/4 c. snipped parsley
1 tsp. dried basil, crushed

COMBINE turkey, bouillon, bay leaf and 7 cups water.
BRING to boiling. Reduce heat.
COVER; simmer 1 hour.
REMOVE turkey carcass; cool.
REMOVE meat from bones and chop.
DISCARD bones.
STRAIN broth.
RETURN broth and turkey to pan.
STIR in cabbage, undrained tomatoes, beans, onion, garlic, parsley,
basil and 1/8 teaspoon pepper.
BRING to boiling; reduce heat.
COVER and simmer 25 to 30 minutes.
YIELD: 6 servings.

Mushroom-Rice Soup

1 med. onion, chopped	1 c. whipping cream
2 tsp. butter	Dash of black pepper
1/2 lb. fresh mushrooms,	Pinch of nutmeg
sliced	1/4 c. cooked rice
2 to 3 T. all-purpose flour	1/4 c. vermouth or sherry (opt.)
4 c. beef consommé	

SAUTÉ onion in butter in 4-quart saucepan until onion is browned.

ADD mushrooms to onion and sauté until tender.

STIR in flour, mixing to coat mushrooms.

COOK for 5 minutes over medium-high heat, stirring occasionally to prevent burning.

ADD cream, black pepper, nutmeg and rice, blending well; do not boil.

REDUCE heat and simmer for 10 minutes.

STIR in vermouth just before serving.

YIELD: 6 cups.

Oyster Bisque

1/4 c. butter or margarine	1 T. Worcestershire sauce
3 garlic cloves, minced	1/8 tsp. hot sauce
2 green onions, finely chopped	1/4 tsp. freshly-ground pepper
3 T. all-purpose flour	1 qt. whipping cream
1 (8 oz) btl. clam juice	2 (12 oz.) ctn. fresh oysters,
1/2 c. dry sherry	drained
1/4 c. lemon juice	

MELT butter in a large Dutch oven. Add garlic and green onion; sauté until tender.

ADD flour; cook 1 minute.

ADD clam juice, sherry and lemon juice; cook 2 minutes or until thickened.

STIR in Worcestershire sauce and the next 3 ingredients. Add oysters and cook, stirring occasionally, 10 minutes or until done.

YIELD: 9 cups.

Potato/Cheese Soup

4 med. potatoes, peeled	1 1/2 tsp. salt
1 med. onion, sliced	Pepper
4 c. boiling water	2 T. butter or margarine
1/3 c. diced summer sausage	1/2 c. grated sharp Cheddar cheese
1/2 tsp. thyme leaves	1 T. grated Parmesan cheese
1/2 tsp. marjoram leaves	

CUT potatoes in halves. Cook with onion in 2 cups boiling water, until tender. Do not drain.

MASH potatoes. Add sausage, thyme, marjoram, salt, pepper, butter, sharp cheese and remaining boiling water.

SIMMER 10 minutes.

ADD grated Parmesan cheese just before serving.

YIELD: 6 servings.

Soups

Potato Soup with Dumplings

SOUP:

1 c. diced celery	1 med. onion, chopped
1/2 c. water	2 tsp. salt
6 med. potatoes	1/4 tsp. pepper
2 c. water	3 c. milk

COOK celery in 1/2 cup water just until tender. Do not drain.

PEEL and cube potatoes.

PLACE in 4-quart saucepan with 2 cups water. Add cooked celery, onion, salt and pepper.

COOK until potatoes are tender. Mash potatoes slightly, to eliminate definite cubes.

ADD milk; set aside until dumplings are mixed.

DUMPLINGS:	1/2 tsp. sugar
1 c. sifted flour	1 tsp. parsley flakes
1 1/2 tsp. baking powder	1 egg
1/2 tsp. salt	1/2 c. milk

SIFT together flour, baking powder, salt and sugar; stir in parsley flakes.

BEAT eggs; add milk. Add to dry ingredients and mix just until moistened.

BRING soup to a boil. Drop dumplings by tablespoonfuls into liquid, so they don't touch.

TURN heat to simmer. Cover tightly. Simmer gently 20 minutes. Don't lift lid!

YIELD: 6 servings.

Pumpkin Soup

2 T. butter
1/4 c. green pepper
2 T. chopped onion
1 lg. sprig parsley
1/8 tsp. thyme leaves
1 bay leaf
1 (8 oz.) can tomatoes

1 (1 lb.) can pumpkin
2 c. chicken broth or stock
1 T. flour
1 c. milk
1 tsp. salt
1/8 tsp. pepper

MELT butter in a large saucepan. Add green pepper, onion, parsley, thyme and bay leaf; cook 5 minutes.
ADD tomatoes, pumpkin and chicken broth; cover and simmer 30 minutes, stirring occasionally.
PRESS mixture through a food mill or wire strainer.
BLEND together flour and milk; stir into soup.
ADD salt and pepper. Cook, stirring frequently, until mixture comes to a boil.
SERVE immediately.
YIELD: 6 servings.

Sausage/Bean Soup

1 1/2 lb. smoked sausage
   links, cut in pieces
1 c. thin-sliced carrots
1 c. thin-sliced celery
1 (1 1/2 oz.) pkg. dry onion
   soup mix
2 T. sugar
1 tsp. salt

1/4 tsp. oregano
6 c. boiling water
1 (28 oz.) can tomatoes
1 (5 1/2 oz.) pkg. hash brown
   potatoes, thawed
1 (10 oz.) pkg. frozen green
   beans
1/4 tsp. Tabasco sauce

IN a 4- to 6-quart Dutch oven, combine sausage, carrots, celery, soup mix, sugar and salt.

ADD boiling water. Stir and heat to boiling. Reduce heat and simmer, covered, for 10 minutes.

MIX in tomatoes, breaking up with a large spoon.

ADD potatoes, green beans, oregano, and Tabasco sauce; heat to boiling.

REDUCE heat and simmer, covered, 30 minutes or until vegetables are tender, stirring occasionally.

GOOD served with a crusty bread.

YIELD: 3 quarts.

Spicy Chicken Soup

1 (2 1/2 to 3 lb.) broiler or
   fryer
1 T. salt
1/2 c. butter or margarine
1 qt. boiling water
1 lg. potato, cubed

1 med. onion, chopped coarsely
2 (17 oz.) cans cream-style corn
1 (15 oz.) can tomatoes, drained
1 (10 oz.) can tomatoes with
   green chilies, undrained
1/2 tsp. pepper

COMBINE chicken, salt, butter and boiling water; bring to a boil, reduce heat and cook until chicken is tender.

REMOVE chicken from broth; let cool and remove meat from bones.

ADD potatoes and onion to broth.

BRING to a boil; reduce heat and cook vegetables until tender.

ADD chicken and remaining ingredients. Simmer 30 to 45 minutes, stirring occasionally.

YIELD: 8 servings.

Soups

Split Pea/Vegetable Soup

1 lb. dried split peas (2 c.)　　1/2 tsp. pepper
3 qt. water　　　　　　　　　1/4 tsp. marjoram leaves
1 meaty ham bone, or if you　　1 1/2 c. chopped onions
　　prefer, 1 1/2 lb. ham hocks　3/4 c. chopped carrots
2 tsp. salt　　　　　　　　　3/4 c. chopped celery

COMBINE peas and water in large soup kettle.
BRING to a boil. Simmer 2 minutes.
REMOVE from heat, cover and let stand 1 hour.
ADD ham bone, salt, pepper, marjoram and onions.
COVER and simmer 1 1/2 hours.
ADD carrots and celery. Continue simmering until tender, 30 to 40 minutes.
ADD more salt if needed.
SERVE hot.
GARNISH with parsley and sliced Polish sausages on top of soup.
YIELD: 3 1/2 quarts.

Turkey-Barley Soup

1 turkey carcass　　　　　　1 c. barley
6 qt. water　　　　　　　　2 (16 oz.) cans tomatoes, drained
12 peppercorns　　　　　　　　& chopped
3 or 4 stalks celery, cut　　　1 c. chopped onion
　　in fourths　　　　　　　1 c. chopped celery
2 bay leaves　　　　　　　　1 c. chopped carrots
1 lg. onion, cut into eighths　　2 tsp. salt
Pinch of garlic powder　　　　1/4 tsp. pepper

COMBINE the first 7 ingredients in a large Dutch oven; bring to a boil. Cover, reduce heat and simmer 1 hour. Remove carcass from broth and pick meat from bones; set aside.
MEASURE 4 quarts broth and return it to Dutch oven. Refrigerate remaining broth for other uses. Bring broth to a boil. Add barley; reduce heat to medium and cook 45 minutes.
ADD turkey, tomatoes and remaining ingredients; simmer 30 minutes. Remove bay leaves.
YIELD: about 5 quarts.

Soups

Turkey Chowder

Vegetable cooking spray
1 sm. onion, chopped
1 c. turkey or chicken broth
1 (8 3/4 oz.) can cream-style corn
1 med. potato, peeled & cubed
1/2 c. chopped celery
1 c. cubed, cooked turkey

1/4 tsp. salt
Dash of pepper
1/8 tsp. paprika
1/8 tsp. ground ginger
1/2 c. milk
1 c. half & half
1 tsp. dried parsley

COAT a large, nonstick skillet with cooking spray. Place over medium-high heat until hot. Add onion and sauté until tender. Add broth and the next 4 ingredients; bring to a boil.

COVER, reduce heat and simmer 20 minutes or until potatoes are tender. Add seasonings. Gradually stir milk and half & half into soup. COOK over low heat until soup is heated through, stirring occasionally. Ladle into bowls and sprinkle with parsley.

YIELD: 1 quart.

Turkey-Corn Chowder

4 med. onions, sliced
1/4 c. butter or margarine
5 med. potatoes, cubed
2 celery stalks, chopped
1 T. salt
1/2 tsp. pepper
1 chicken bouillon cube
2 c. water
5 c. milk

2 (15 1/4 oz.) cans whole kernel
   corn, drained
1 (14 3/4 oz.) can cream-style
   corn
1 c. half & half
1 1/2 tsp. paprika
1/4 tsp. dried thyme
3 c. cooked, chopped turkey
Chopped fresh parsley (or dried)

SAUTÉ onion in butter in a Dutch oven until tender.
ADD cubed potato and the next 5 ingredients; bring to a boil.
COVER, reduce heat and simmer 15 minutes or until vegetables are tender.
ADD milk and the next 6 ingredients; cook until heated.
SPRINKLE with parsley.
YIELD: 5 quarts.

Soups

Turkey Frame Soup

How to have a happy ending for your festive holiday bird!

1 meaty turkey frame	8 c. fresh vegetables*
1 med. onion, quartered	1 recipe old-fashioned egg
3 med. tomatoes, quartered	noodles
1 tsp. dried thyme, crushed	4 tsp. salt
1/2 tsp. dried oregano, crushed	

PLACE turkey frame in a large Dutch oven or kettle with 5 quarts water, onion and salt. Bring to boiling.
REDUCE heat. Simmer, covered, 1 1/2 hours.
REMOVE frame; cook until easy to handle.
REMOVE meat from bones; discard bones. Strain broth.
RETURN meat to broth with tomatoes, thyme and oregano.
STIR in vegetables.
BRING to boiling; cover and simmer 45 minutes. Add noodles.
BOIL 15 minutes.
YIELD: 12 servings.

NOTE: Vegetables may be any combination you choose: chopped celery, carrot, onion, rutabaga, broccoli, shredded cabbage and cauliflowerets.

NOODLES:

1 beaten egg	1 to 1 1/4 c. all-purpose flour
2 T. milk	1/2 tsp. salt

IN mixing bowl, combine egg, milk and salt.
ADD enough of the flour to make a stiff dough (do not use too much flour at the beginning, remember, you can always add more).
ROLL dough thinly on floured surface (be sure you have enough flour on your rolling surface, but don't start with too much; add as you need).
LET stand 20 minutes. Roll up loosely. Slice 1/4-inch wide.
UNROLL cut noodles; spread out. Let dry 2 hours.
COOK in soup.

NOODLES seem to intimidate a lot of people, but are not that hard to make. This is the easiest recipe I have found. Even if the first attempt isn't what you wish it to be, you'll find it better every time you try.

Soups

Turkey-Noodle Soup

1 turkey carcass	1 tsp. salt
4 qt. water	1/4 tsp. pepper
1/2 c. finely-chopped onion	4 oz. med. egg noodles
1/2 c. finely-chopped celery	uncooked

PLACE turkey carcass and water in a large Dutch oven; bring to a boil. Cover, reduce heat and simmer 1 hour. Remove carcass from broth and pick meat from bones. Set meat aside.
MEASURE 8 cups broth and refrigerate remainder for other uses.
ADD onion and the next 3 ingredients to broth in Dutch oven. Bring to a boil, cover, reduce heat and simmer 1 hour. Stir in turkey and noodles. Simmer, uncovered, 8 minutes or until noodles are tender.
YIELD: 2 quarts.

Wild Rice Soup From Minnesota

People from Minnesota seem to be experts on wild rice soup, this is the best I have ever eaten.

1/2 c. minced onion	1 c. half & half or whipping
1/4 c. finely-chopped celery	cream
1/4 c. finely-chopped carrots	1 c. cooked wild rice (not instant
2 T. butter	or precooked)
1 1/2 c. sliced fresh mushrooms	1/8 tsp. bitters
1/4 c. all-purpose flour	3/4 tsp. dried chervil
3/4 tsp. salt	2 T. brandy or dry white wine
1/4 tsp. freshly-ground pepper	1/4 c. blanched sliced almonds
2 c. beef broth	

SAUTÉ onion, celery and carrots in butter in 3-quart saucepan for 3 minutes or until onion is softened.
ADD mushrooms and cook over low heat for 3 to 4 minutes.
SIFT flour, salt and pepper into vegetables.
COOK, while stirring, until mixture is bubbly and golden brown.
ADD broth and half & half, whisking to blend, and cook over low heat until thickened and smooth.
STIR in wild rice, bitters, chervil, brandy and almonds.
HEAT thoroughly over low heat; do not scorch.
YIELD: 6 cups.

Soups

MEATS

List Your Favorite Recipes

Recipes   **Page**

_____   _____

_____   _____

_____   _____

_____   _____

_____   _____

_____   _____

_____   _____

_____   _____

_____   _____

_____   _____

_____   _____

_____   _____

_____   _____

_____   _____

_____   _____

_____   _____

_____   _____

_____   _____

Apple-Walnut Stuffing

1/3 c. butter or margarine	1 c. chopped walnuts
1 lg. onion, finely chopped	2 T. diced whole-leaf sage
2 stalks celery, finely chopped	1/2 tsp. dried rosemary
1 c. chopped red cooking apple	1/2 tsp. dried thyme
1 c. chopped green cooking apple	1 lg. egg, beaten
	1/2 c. milk
2 c. white bread cubes, toasted	1/2 tsp. salt & pepper

MELT butter in a small skillet over medium-high heat. Add onion and celery. Cook, stirring constantly, until tender.

COMBINE apples, bread cubes and the next 4 ingredients in a large bowl. Stir in vegetable mixture, egg and remaining ingredients. Spoon into lightly-greased 7 x 11 x 1 1/2-inch baking dish.

BAKE at 350° for 30 minutes.

YIELD: 6 servings.

Meats

Baked Burgundy Ham

1 (6 to 8 lb.) smoked fully-
    cooked ham half, well
    trimmed
6 c. water
2 c. cranberry juice cocktail,
    divided

2 c. dry red wine, divided
2 c. firmly-packed dark brown
    sugar, divided
2 (3") sticks cinnamon
1 T. whole cloves

PLACE ham in a large Dutch oven.
ADD water, 1 cup cranberry juice cocktail, 1 cup wine, 1 cup brown
sugar, cinnamon sticks and cloves.
BRING to a boil, cover, reduce heat and simmer 20 minutes. Cool.
REMOVE ham and marinade from Dutch oven and place in a large
nonmetallic bowl.
COVER and chill 8 hours, turning once.
REMOVE ham from marinade. Reserve 2 cups marinade.
DISCARD remaining marinade.
PLACE ham in a lightly-greased shallow roasting pan; cover.
BAKE at 325° for 1 1/2 hours, basting ham occasionally with reserved
marinade.
UNCOVER and bake 15 additional minutes or until meat thermom-
eter registers 140°, basting ham occasionally with pan juices.
REMOVE ham, reserving pan juice.
COMBINE pan juices, remaining 1 cup cranberry juice, 1 cup wine
and 1 cup brown sugar in a saucepan.
BRING to a boil, reduce heat and cook 20 minutes.
SERVE with ham.
YIELD: 12 to 14 servings.

Chicken-Cheese Rosettes

4 med. chicken breasts, skinned & boned
1 med. onion, finely chopped
8 oz. fresh mushrooms, sliced
1/4 c. butter or margarine
3/4 c. dry white wine
1/2 tsp. dried tarragon, crushed
1/2 tsp. salt
1/2 tsp. white pepper
8 lasagna noodles, cooked & drained
1 (8 oz.) pkg. cream cheese, cut up
1/2 c. light cream or milk
1/2 c. dairy sour cream
1 1/2 c. shredded Gruyére cheese (6 oz.)
1 c. shredded Muenster cheese (4 oz.)
1 whole almond
3 T. slivered almonds, toasted
Snipped parsley

CUT chicken into 1-inch pieces. In a 10-inch skillet, cook onion and mushrooms in butter or margarine until tender, but not brown.
ADD chicken, wine, tarragon, salt and pepper.
BRING to boiling; reduce heat.
COVER and simmer for 8 to 10 minutes or until chicken is tender.
MEANWHILE, halve lasagna noodles lengthwise.
CURL each into a 2 1/2-inch-diameter ring and place in a 9x13x2-inch baking dish.
USING a slotted spoon, spoon chicken-mushroom mixture into center of lasagna rings.
TO broth in the skillet, add cream cheese, light cream or milk, sour cream, half of Gruyére and half of the Muenster cheese.
COOK and stir until cheeses are melted (do not boil). Pour over lasagna rings.
INSERT a whole almond in one of the rings.
SPRINKLE remaining cheeses and slivered almonds over rings.
BAKE, covered, in a 325° oven for 35 minutes.
GARNISH with parsley.
YIELD: 8 servings.

Chicken Pastries

These are wonderful for a holiday buffet.

1 (17 1/4 oz.) pkg. frozen
    puff pastry sheets, thawed
1/2 c. cream cheese (mixed
    with 1/4 tsp. onion powder
    and 1/8 tsp. dried chives)
6 skinned & boned chicken
    breast halves (may use
    turkey)

1/2 tsp. salt
1/8 tsp. pepper
1 egg, beaten
1 T. water
Garnish: green leaves, kale or
    lettuce

UNFOLD pastry sheets and roll each sheet into a 12x14-inch rectangle on a lightly-floured surface.

CUT 1 sheet into 4 (6x7-inch) rectangles. Cut second sheet into 2 (6x7-inch) rectangles and 1 (6x12-inch) rectangle. Set large rectangle aside.

SHAPE each small rectangle into an oval by trimming off corners.

SPREAD pastry ovals evenly with cream cheese mixture.

SPRINKLE chicken breasts with salt and pepper and place in center of each pastry oval.

LIGHTLY moisten pastry edges with water.

FOLD ends over chicken. Fold sides over, and press to seal.

PLACE bundle, seam-side down, onto a lightly-greased baking sheet.

CUT remaining large pastry rectangle into 12 x 1/4-inch strips.

BRAID 2 strips together and place crosswise over chicken bundles, trimming and reserving excess braid; braid 2 additional strips and place lengthwise over bundle, trimming and tucking ends under.

REPEAT procedure with remaining strips.

COVER and refrigerate up to 2 hours, if desired.

COMBINE egg and 1 tablespoon water; brush over pastry bundles.

BAKE at 400° on lower oven rack, 25 minutes or until golden brown.

GARNISH, if desired.

YIELD: 6 servings.

Meats

Christmas Ham

1 whole bone-in fully-cooked
   spiral-cut ham (this makes
   your dinner so much easier)
2 (6 oz.) cans pineapple juice

1 (20 oz.) can crushed pineapple,
   undrained
2 c. packed brown sugar
About 25 whole cloves
1/4 c. golden raisins

PLACE ham in roasting pan.
SLOWLY pour pineapple juice over ham.
SPOON crushed pineapple over ham.
ADD brown sugar and cloves to top of ham.
ADD raisins to pan.
COVER and refrigerate overnight.
REMOVE cloves; discard.
COVER ham.
BAKE at 325° for 1 1/2 hours to 2 hours, or until meat thermometer
registers 140°. Baste every 20 minutes.
YIELD: 20 to 25 servings.

Cornbread Dressing

2 c. self-rising flour	1 or 2 med. onions, chopped
1 c. self-rising cornmeal	1 jalapeño pepper, seeded &
2 c. buttermilk	chopped
3 lg. eggs	1/4 tsp. pepper
1/2 c. butter or margarine,	2 to 3 c. chicken broth
melted	Paprika
Vegetable cooking spray	Celery leaves, for garnish
1 c. chopped celery	

COMBINE flour and cornmeal in a large bowl. Make a well in center of flour mixture.

COMBINE eggs and buttermilk, stirring well. Add to dry ingredients, stirring until moistened.

PLACE a 9-inch square baking pan in a 400° oven for 5 minutes or until hot.

REMOVE pan from oven and coat with cooking spray.

SPOON batter into hot baking pan.

BAKE at 400° for 25 minutes or until lightly browned.

COOL in pan on a wire rack and crumble cornbread into a large bowl.

ADD celery and the next 3 ingredients, stirring well.

STIR in enough chicken broth to make a moist, thick mixture. Spoon into a 7 x 11 x 1 1/2-inch baking dish coated with vegetable cooking spray.

BAKE at 350° for 20 minutes or until lightly browned.

SPRINKLE with paprika and garnish, if desired.

YIELD: 8 servings.

Cornish Game Hens with Wild Rice Dressing

2 (1 1/2 lb.) Cornish game hens, halved lengthwise	1/4 c. regular brown rice
1/2 c. chopped onion	1/4 tsp. ground sage
1 T. margarine or butter	1/4 tsp. dried oregano, crushed
1 3/4 c. chicken broth	1/8 tsp. pepper
1/2 c. wild rice	1 c. shredded carrot
	Melted margarine or butter

RINSE hen halves. Twist wing tips under backs.

COVER and chill.

FOR stuffing, cook onion in margarine or butter until tender.

STIR in broth, wild rice, brown rice, ground sage, oregano and pepper.

BRING to boiling; reduce heat.

SIMMER, covered, for 40 to 50 minutes or until liquid is absorbed.

STIR in carrot.

COOL; cover and chill for up to 24 hours.

TO bake, spoon rice stuffing into 4 mounds on bottom of a 9x13x2-inch baking dish.

PLACE Cornish hens, cut-side down, over rice mounds.

BRUSH with melted margarine.

BAKE at 375° for 45 minutes.

UNCOVER; brush hens with melted margarine.

BAKE, uncovered, for 30 to 35 minutes more, or until tender.

ARRANGE hens on top of rice stuffing on 4 plates.

GARNISH with a sprig of fresh sage, if desired.

YIELD: 4 servings.

Cranberry-Apple Stuffing

1/2 c. butter	2 red tart apples, cored & chopped
2 c. chopped celery	1 1/4 c. dried cranberries
1/2 c. chopped onion	1 tsp. fresh grated orange peel
1 tsp. thyme leaves	(opt.)
1 tsp. rosemary leaves	4 c. unseasoned dry bread crumbs
1 tsp. parsley flakes	1 c. chicken broth

PREHEAT oven to 325°.
IN a skillet, melt butter. Add celery and onion; sauté 5 minutes.
REMOVE from heat. Stir in the next 5 ingredients, and orange peel, if desired.
PLACE bread cubes in a large bowl; stir in fruit mixture.
ADD broth; toss to combine.
PLACE in a 9x13-inch baking dish.
COVER and bake 35 to 40 minutes.
YIELD: 8 cups.

Cranberry Relish

1 lg. orange	2 c. sugar
1 lg. lemon	1/2 c. dry sherry
4 c. fresh cranberries	

REMOVE the peel from the orange and lemon, reserving half the peel from each.
REMOVE excess white membrane from reserved peels; discard membrane.
PLACE fruit pulp, peels and cranberries through the coarse blade of a food grinder, or coarse-chop of a food processor.
ADD sugar and dry sherry; mix thoroughly.
LET stand 30 minutes at room temperature; stir again.
LADLE into jars or freezer containers; cover.
REFRIGERATE or freeze.
YIELD: 4 1/2 cups.

Currant Jelly-Glazed Pork Roast

4 or 5 lb. boneless pork loin
    roast (double loin, rolled,
    tied)
1 (10 oz.) jar currant jelly

1/3 c. light corn syrup
2 T. cider vinegar
1/2 tsp. dry mustard
1/4 tsp. ginger

PLACE roast on rack in shallow roasting pan.

INSERT meat thermometer so bulb is in the center of thickest part of roast.

ROAST, uncovered, in 325° oven about 2 1/2 to 3 hours, or until meat thermometer registers 170°.

WHILE roast is cooking, prepare glaze.

COMBINE jelly, corn syrup, vinegar, dry mustard and ginger in saucepan.

BRING to simmering stage; simmer 2 minutes.

BRUSH glaze over roast several times during the last 30 minutes of cooking time.

YIELD: 8 to 10 servings.

GARNISH, if desired, with fresh holly and cherry tomatoes.

Dijon-Rosemary Lamb Chops

1/4 c. Dijon mustard	2 T. olive oil
8 lamb chops (4 lb.)	1 c. dry white wine, divided
1 T. dried rosemary, crushed	1/2 c. whipping cream
All-purpose flour	Salt & pepper

SPREAD mustard over lamb chops; sprinkle evenly with rosemary.
DREDGE chops in flour, shaking off excess flour.
POUR oil in a large skillet; place over medium-high heat until hot.
ADD chops and cook until browned, turning once.
REDUCE heat to medium; cover and cook 10 minutes.
TURN chops over and add 1/4 cup dry white wine.
COOK an additional 10 minutes or to desired degree of doneness.
REMOVE chops from skillet and keep warm.
ADD remaining 3/4 cup wine to pan drippings, stirring to loosen browned particles.
COOK, stirring occasionally, 10 minutes or until liquid is reduced to about 1 cup.
ADD whipping cream; simmer 2 minutes.
SEASON with salt and pepper, to taste.
SERVE sauce with lamb chops.
YIELD: 4 servings.

Fruitcake-Stuffed Pork Loin

1/3 c. chopped onion	1 c. chicken broth
1 clove garlic, minced	1/4 c. bourbon
1 T. olive oil	1/4 c. honey
3 c. crumbled fruitcake	2 T. butter or margarine
1 (5 lb.) boneless rolled pork	2 T. all-purpose flour
loin roast	2 T. bourbon
1/4 tsp. salt	1/4 c. whipping cream
1/4 tsp. pepper	Garnishes: fresh grapes, thyme
2 T. dried thyme, divided	sprigs, canned crab apples
1 c. apple juice	

COOK onion and garlic in olive oil in a skillet over medium-high heat, stirring constantly, until tender. Remove skillet from heat; add fruitcake and stir well.

REMOVE pork loin from elastic net (there should be 2 pieces). Trim excess fat. Make a cut lengthwise down the center of each piece, cutting to, but not through bottom. Starting from center cut of each piece, slice horizontally toward 1 side, stopping 1/2-inch from edge. Repeat on opposite side. Unfold each piece of meat so that it lies flat.

FLATTEN to 1/2-inch thickness, using a meat mallet or rolling pin.

SPRINKLE salt, pepper and 1 tablespoon thyme evenly over pork. Sprinkle fruitcake mixture over pork.

ROLL each loin half, jellyroll-fashion, starting with long side. Secure with string and place, seam-side down, in a shallow roasting pan.

POUR apple juice and chicken broth around rolled pork loins in pan.

COMBINE 1/4 cup bourbon and honey. Brush lightly over rolled pork loins. Sprinkle with remaining tablespoon thyme.

BAKE at 350° for 50 minutes or until meat thermometer inserted in thickest portion registers 160°, basting with bourbon mixture at 20-minute intervals. Remove pork loins from pan, reserving pan drippings; keep pork warm.

POUR pan drippings into a saucepan; bring to a boil and cook about 10 to 15 minutes, until mixture is reduced to 1 cup; set aside.

MELT butter in a heavy saucepan over low heat. Add flour, stirring until smooth. Cook 1 minute, stirring constantly. Gradually add reduced drippings and 2 tablespoons bourbon; cook over medium heat, stirring constantly until mixture thickens and boils. Remove from heat; stir in whipping cream. Garnish pork, if desired. Serve sauce with sliced pork. YIELD: 10 servings.

Meats

Fruited Holiday Pork Roast

3 lb. pork roast
1 c. red cooking wine
1/2 c. honey
1 c. cranberries

1/2 c. cranberry juice
1 tsp. dry mustard
1/2 c. apricot preserves
1/2 tsp. pepper

MIX all ingredients and place over roast.
ROAST, covered, at 350° until meat thermometer registers 180° to 185°, about 2 to 2 1/2 hours.

Giblet Gravy

1 T. olive oil
Turkey giblets: neck, heart, gizzard & liver
2 stalks celery, roughly chopped
1 carrot, peeled & roughly chopped
1 leek, trimmed & roughly chopped

1 c. white wine
4 c. homemade turkey or chicken stock, may use canned
6 whole black peppercorns
1 bay leaf
3 T. all-purpose flour
Salt & freshly-ground pepper, to taste
1 c. Madeira

HEAT olive oil in medium saucepan over medium-high heat.
ADD giblets; cook, stirring, until browned on all sides.
REMOVE giblets; set aside.
REDUCE heat to medium; add celery, carrot and leek. Cook, stirring, until leeks begin to brown, about 10 minutes.
ADD white wine and Madeira; cook until reduced by half, about 15 to 20 minutes.
ADD stock, giblets, peppercorns and bay leaf. Simmer for 40 minutes. Strain; discard solids.
POUR juices from pan into fat separator; let separate, about 10 minutes.
PLACE roasting pan over medium heat; add turkey juices, reserving fat. Scrape bottom and sides with a wooden spoon to dislodge any brown bits.
ADD 3 tablespoons turkey fat and flour; cook, stirring, until brown, about 2 minutes.
WHISK in strained stock, 1 cup at a time, until incorporated.
REMOVE from heat; strain into saucepan.
OVER medium-high heat, cook until thickened, 10 to 15 minutes.
Season to taste with salt and pepper. Serve.
YIELD: 2 cups.

Meats

Ham Brioche

3 T. butter	1/2 tsp. salt
1/2 lb. button mushrooms	2 T. melted butter
2 T. green onions, minced	3 T. flour
1 T. lemon juice	3 c. cooked, diced ham
1/4 c. dry sherry	1/2 c. stuffed green olives, cut in
2 c. heavy cream	half

MELT 3 tablespoons of butter in a large pan.

ADD green onions and mushrooms; cover with lemon juice.

COVER and cook 2 to 3 minutes. Add sherry, cream and salt; bring to a boil.

BLEND 2 tablespoons melted butter with 3 tablespoons flour until smooth, and add gradually to cream mixture. Cook, stirring constantly, until thickened.

ADD ham and olives; cook over low heat until heated through. Season with salt to taste, if you feel you need more. You may add ground pepper, and a little basil.

YIELD: 4 to 6 servings.

THIS is a great buffet dish, very creamy and delicious.

Herb-Roasted Turkey and Potatoes

1 1/2 lb. boneless turkey breast	4 red potatoes, quartered
1 clove garlic, thinly sliced	3/4 tsp. onion salt
2 T. margarine, melted	3/4 tsp. dried oregano
	Paprika

CUT slits in surface of turkey and insert garlic slices.

PLACE turkey, skin-side up, in a 9x13x2-inch baking pan.

PLACE potatoes around the turkey.

DRIZZLE potatoes with margarine.

COMBINE onion salt and oregano.

SPRINKLE over turkey and potatoes.

SEASON potatoes with paprika.

BAKE at 350° for 1 1/2 hours, or until internal temperature of turkey is 170°.

LET stand 5 minutes before slicing.

YIELD: 6 servings.

Meats

Holiday Roasted Lamb

3/4 tsp. dried rosemary, crushed	1/2 tsp. whole cloves
1/2 tsp. garlic powder	1/4 tsp. ground ginger
1/3 c. sugar	3 med. apples, cored & sliced
1/3 c. vinegar	1/2 c. packed brown sugar
3 T. light corn syrup	1/3 c. frozen orange juice concentrate, thawed
3 T. water	2 tsp. prepared mustard
2" stick cinnamon	3/4 tsp. ground cinnamon

COMBINE rosemary and garlic powder.

RUB over lamb.

PLACE lamb on a rack in a shallow roasting pan.

INSERT a meat thermometer in the thickest portion of the meat.

ROAST, uncovered, in a 325° oven for 2 1/4 to 2 1/2 hours or until meat thermometer registers 160°.

MEANWHILE, in a medium skillet, combine sugar, vinegar, corn syrup, water, stick cinnamon, cloves and ginger.

BRING to boiling.

REDUCE heat and simmer, covered, for 4 minutes.

ADD apple slices and simmer for 4 minutes.

REMOVE apple slices.

RESERVE 2 tablespoons poaching liquid.

HALVE 4 or 5 of the apple slices. Set aside.

FOR glaze, combine brown sugar, orange juice concentrate, mustard, ground cinnamon and reserved poaching liquid.

REMOVE roast from the oven.

CUT 3-inch slits in the top of roast.

INSERT halved apple slices in slits.

SPOON some of the glaze over roast.

RETURN roast to oven and roast for 20 minutes more, spooning glaze over top once or twice.

TO serve, arrange remaining apple slices on a serving platter with roast.

DRIZZLE any remaining glaze over meat.

GARNISH with parsley sprigs, if desired.

YIELD: 10 servings.

Leftover Holiday Casserole

1 (7 oz.) pkg. spaghetti, cooked
1 3/4 c. (7 oz.) shredded Monterey Jack cheese
1 1/2 c. chopped cooked turkey
1 (2 oz.) jar diced pimento, undrained
1 sm. green bell pepper, chopped
1 sm. onion, chopped
1 (10 3/4 oz.) can cream of celery soup, undiluted
1/2 c. chicken broth
1/2 tsp. salt
1/4 tsp. pepper

COMBINE spaghetti, 1 1/4 cups cheese, turkey and the next 7 ingredients, stirring gently. Spoon mixture into a lightly-greased 7x11-inch baking dish, or you may spray with nonstick vegetable coating.
SPRINKLE with remaining 1/2 cup cheese.
BAKE at 350° for 45 minutes or until bubbly.
YIELD: 8 servings.

Lemon-Currant Glazed Ham

1 (2 to 2 1/2 lb.) fully-cooked boneless ham	1/4 c. chicken broth
1/2 c. red currant jelly	2 tsp. cornstarch
1/4 c. dry red wine	Steamed green onion tops
1 T. lemon juice	Orange peel, cut into thin strips

USE a sharp knife to make diagonal cuts about 1/2-inch deep and 1-inch apart in the top of ham.

PLACE ham on a rack in a shallow baking pan.

INSERT a meat thermometer in the center of the thickest portion of meat.

BAKE, uncovered, in a 325° oven for 1 1/2 to 2 hours or until thermometer registers 140°.

MEANWHILE, for glaze, in a small saucepan, combine jelly, 2 tablespoons of the wine and lemon juice.

COOK and stir until jelly is melted.

AFTER ham has baked about 1 1/4 hours, brush with half of the glaze.

FOR sauce, in a small bowl, stir together remaining wine, chicken broth and cornstarch.

STIR into remaining glaze in saucepan.

COOK and stir until thickened and bubbly.

COOK and stir 2 minutes more.

TRANSFER ham to a serving platter.

GARNISH with green onion tops and orange peel in a crisscross pattern.

SERVE with sauce.

YIELD: 8 to 10 servings.

Pork Chops with
Sweet Potatoes and Apples

4 (1/2" thick) boneless
   butterflied pork chops
1 c. apple cider, divided
4 sweet potatoes, peeled &
   cut into 1/2" thick slices
1 tsp. cornstarch

1 T. dried sage leaves, crumbled
3/4 tsp. salt
1/4 tsp. pepper
2 lg. Rome or other cooking
   apples, cored & sliced

BROWN pork chops on both sides in a nonstick skillet.

BRING to a boil; cover, reduce heat and simmer 10 minutes.

ADD apple and pork chops; cover and simmer 10 to 15 minutes or until sweet potato is tender and pork chops are done.

REMOVE apple, sweet potato and pork chops to serving plate, reserving drippings in skillet.

COMBINE remaining 1/4 cup cider with cornstarch, stirring until smooth.

STIR into drippings.

COOK over medium heat, stirring constantly, until mixture thickens and boils.

BOIL, stirring constantly, 1 minute.

POUR over pork chops.

YIELD: 4 servings.

Pork Scallopini

1 lb. pork cutlets, 1/4" thick	1/4 c. dry white wine
Salt & freshly-ground pepper	1/4 c. water or chicken broth
1/4 c. flour	1/2 T. dried parsley, or 1 T. fresh
1 T. butter	chopped parsley
1 T. oil	

POUND cutlets to the 1/4-inch thickness.

SEASON with salt and pepper, to taste.

DIP in flour and shake off excess.

IN a large frying pan, heat butter and oil.

ADD pork pieces, browning them for about 3 minutes each side.

REMOVE pork to a heated plate.

ADD wine and water (or broth) to pan, stirring and scraping up browned bits.

RETURN pork to pan and simmer over low heat, covered, for 5 to 6 minutes.

TRANSFER to heated platter. Add sauce and parsley garnish.

SERVE with green beans, brown rice and a spinach salad.

Rack of Lamb with Cherry-Wine Sauce

2 (8-rib) lamb rib roasts,
    trimmed (2 3/4 to 3 lb.
    each)
3 to 4 T. coarse-grained
    Dijon mustard
1/3 c. fine, dry bread crumbs
1/3 c. finely-chopped hazelnuts

1/4 c. finely-chopped parsley
1/2 tsp. finely-ground pepper
1 tsp. dried thyme
1/4 tsp. salt
Cherry-Wine Sauce (recipe
    below)

PLACE lamb roasts in a roasting pan, fat-side out and ribs criss-crossed (sliced with sharp knife).
SPREAD mustard over roasts.
COMBINE bread crumbs and the next 5 ingredients; pat over roasts.
INVERT meat thermometer into thickest portion of lamb, making sure it does not touch fat or bone.
BAKE at 400° for 10 minutes; shield exposed bones with strips of foil to prevent excessive browning.
REDUCE heat to 375° and bake 30 additional minutes or until meat thermometer registers 145°.
REMOVE from oven, cover loosely with foil and let stand 5 minutes or until meat thermometer registers 150° (medium-rare).
SERVE with Cherry-Wine Sauce.
YIELD: 5 to 8 servings.

CHERRY-WINE SAUCE:

2/3 c. dry red wine
1/3 c. beef broth
3 T. honey
1/2 tsp. dried thyme
1/4 tsp. salt

1/4 tsp. dry mustard
2 tsp. cornstarch
2 T. balsamic vinegar
1 (16 1/2 oz.) can pitted dark
    cherries, drained

COMBINE the first 6 ingredients in a heavy saucepan; bring to a boil.
BOIL 5 minutes.
COMBINE cornstarch and vinegar, stirring well; add to wine mixture.
BRING to a boil over medium-high heat; boil 1 minute.
STIR in cherries.
YIELD: 1 1/2 cups.

Rice Stuffing

1 1/2 c. long-grain rice,
   uncooked
2 1/2 c. chopped onion
1 1/2 c. chopped green onion
   tops
1 1/2 c. chopped red bell
   pepper

1/4 c. bacon drippings
1 tsp. seasoned salt
1 tsp. celery seeds
1/2 tsp. salt
1/2 tsp. pepper
1 T. Worcestershire sauce
1/4 c. chopped fresh parsley

COOK rice according to package directions; set aside.
COOK onion, green onion tops, celery and bell pepper in bacon drippings in a large skillet over medium-high heat, stirring constantly, until tender. Stir in seasoned salt and next 4 ingredients.
COMBINE rice, vegetable mixture and parsley in a serving bowl, tossing gently; serve immediately, or use for stuffing.
YIELD: 8 to 10 servings.

Roast Turkey and Sausage Stuffing

24 c. fresh bread cubes, may use packaged (1 1/2 lb.)
1 1/2 c. finely-chopped celery
1 c. finely-chopped onion
1 c. butter, melted
8 oz. bulk pork sausage, cooked & drained
1/2 c. snipped parsley
1 or 2 T. dried sage, crushed
2 or 3 tsp. dried thyme, crushed
1/4 tsp. salt
1/4 tsp. pepper
1 1/2 to 2 c. chicken stock or broth (may used canned)
1 (12 to 14 lb.) turkey
Cooking oil

FOR stuffing: Spread bread cubes in single layer on baking sheets. Cover loosely with clean towel. Let stand at room temperature to dry overnight.

IN a large skillet, cook celery and onion in butter until tender.

IN a very large bowl, combine the bread cubes and celery mixture. Stir in the sausage, parsley, sage, thyme, salt and pepper. Add enough stock or broth to moisten, tossing lightly.

RINSE turkey on the outside, as well as inside body and neck cavities; pat dry with paper towels. Season body cavity with salt. Spoon some of the stuffing loosely into the neck cavity. Pull the neck skin back; fasten with a skewer. Lightly spoon more stuffing into body cavity. (Place remaining stuffing in casserole alongside turkey, 60 minutes or until heated.)

TUCK ends of drumsticks under band of skin across tail. If there isn't a band, tie drumsticks to tail with string. Twist wing tips under back.

PLACE turkey, breast-side up, on a rack in a shallow roasting pan. Brush with oil. Insert a meat thermometer into center of an inside thigh muscle. Thermometer bulb should not touch bone. Cover turkey loosely with foil.

ROAST the turkey in a 325° oven 3 1/2 to 4 1/2 hours or until thermometer registers 180° to 185°. After 2 1/2 hours, cut the band of skin or string between drumsticks so thighs will cook evenly. When done, drumsticks should move easily in sockets, and their thickest parts should feel soft when pressed. Uncover the last 30 minutes of roasting.

REMOVE the turkey from the oven. Cover; let stand 15 to 20 minutes before carving. Remove stuffing from turkey; place stuffing in a serving bowl. Carve turkey.

YIELD: 14 to 16 servings.

Roast Turkey with Oyster Stuffing

1 (10 to 12 lb.) turkey
1 pt. shucked oysters
1/2 c. chopped celery
1/2 c. chopped onion
1 bay leaf
1/4 c. butter or margarine
6 c. dry bread crumbs
   (about 24 slices)

2 beaten eggs
1 T. snipped parsley
1 tsp. poultry seasoning
1/2 tsp. salt
Dash of pepper
Cooking oil

RINSE turkey; pat dry with paper towel. Sprinkle cavities with salt.
DRAIN oysters, reserving liquid.
CUT up oysters.
FOR stuffing, cook celery, onion and bay leaf in hot butter or margarine until tender, but not brown.
DISCARD bay leaf.
STIR in oysters, bread crumbs, eggs, parsley, poultry seasoning, salt and pepper.
ADD enough reserved oyster liquid to moisten; toss gently to mix..
TO stuff, spoon some of the stuffing loosely into the neck cavity.
PULL neck skin to back; skewer closed.
LOOSELY spoon remaining stuffing into body cavity.
TIE legs to tail.
TWIST wing tips under back.
PLACE bird, breast-side up, onto a rack in a shallow roasting pan.
BRUSH with oil.
INSERT a meat thermometer into the center of the inside thigh muscle, making sure bulb does not touch bone.
ROAST in a 325° oven for 4 to 5 hours, or until the thermometer registers 180° to 185° and drumstick twists easily in socket.
GARNISH turkey with spiced crab apples and parsley, if desired.
YIELD: 12 servings.

Roasted Free-Range Turkey

3/4 c. (1 1/2 sticks) unsalted
    butter
6 ribs celery, strings
    removed, cut in 1/4" dice
2 lg. onions, cut in 1/4" dice
1/4 c. thyme leaves, finely
    chopped
1 T. flat-leaf parsley, chopped
1/2 lb. roasted chestnuts
    (see below)

27 slices stale white bread, crusts
    removed, cut in 1/4" dice
    (about 8 c.), lightly toasted
    (1 1/2 lb.)
1 1/4 c. homemade turkey
    or chicken stock, skimmed of
    fat, may use canned
4 ripe Anjou pears, cored, peeled
    & 1/4" diced
1 T. salt
1 (12 to 14 lb.) free-range turkey

HEAT oven to 375°.

IN large skillet, melt 4 tablespoons butter over medium heat.

ADD celery and onions. Cook, stirring until translucent, about 10 minutes.

STIR in 2 tablespoons thyme, sage, parsley, chestnuts and bread.

ADD stock, 1/2 cup at a time, until bread becomes moist.

STIR in pears; remove from heat.

PLACE remaining 1 stick butter, remaining 2 tablespoons thyme and salt in food processor.

PULSE until well combined; set aside.

WASH turkey and pat dry.

PLACE, breast-side up, on roasting rack set in a large roasting pan.

SEASON turkey cavity with remaining 2 teaspoons salt.

FILL cavity loosely with stuffing.

TIE legs together with string.

FOLD neck flap over; secure with skewers.

RUN reserved thyme-butter mixture all over turkey.

ROAST for 2 1/2 hours, basting often.

BAKE another 30 to 45 minutes, until an instant thermometer placed in thickest part of thigh reads 180°.

IF turkey becomes too brown, tent with aluminum foil.

Continued on following page.

Continued from preceding page.

LET cool for 20 to 30 minutes before carving.

YOU may bake your stuffing in a buttered casserole at 375° for 30 to 45 minutes, or until heated through.

YIELD: 8 to 10 servings.

ROASTED CHESTNUTS: 1 to 2 lb. fresh lg. chestnuts

HEAT oven to 400°.

USING a sharp paring knife or a chestnut knife (kitchen supply stores carry), score each chestnut; either make an X on one side of nut or make one long slit crosswise.

PLACE chestnuts in a single layer on a baking sheet and bake until flesh is tender and golden, about 25 minutes. Remove from the oven.

USING a clean kitchen towel, immediately peel shells and chop for stuffing.

(IF you cannot find chestnuts or simply do not wish to go to the extra work, you can check in some gourmet shops, or replace the chestnuts with chopped walnuts.)

Roast Goose with Apple Stuffing

1 (7 to 9 lb.) domestic goose   3/4 tsp. dried sage, crushed
1 c. chopped onion   1/2 tsp. salt
2 T. butter or margarine   1/8 tsp. pepper
5 c. dry bread cubes   2 beaten eggs
2 c. chopped, peeled apple   1/2 c. chicken broth
1/4 c. snipped parsley

REMOVE liver from goose and chop.
RINSE the goose and pat dry with paper towels.
SET goose aside.
COOK liver and onion in butter or margarine until liver is done and onion is tender.
IN a large bowl, combine liver mixture, bread cubes, apple, parsley, sage, salt and pepper.
STIR together eggs and chicken broth.
ADD egg mixture to bread cube mixture and toss.
LIGHTLY stuff the body cavity of the goose with the bread mixture.
TIE legs to tail.
TWIST wing tips under back.
PRICK legs and wings with fork.
PLACE goose, breast-side up, on a rack in shallow roasting pan.
INSERT meat thermometer in center of inside thigh muscle, making sure bulb does not touch bone.
ROAST the goose at 350° about 2 1/2 hours, or until thermometer registers 185° and the drumstick moves easily in its socket; spoon off fat.
YIELD: 10 to 12 servings.

Meats   105

Roasted Turkey and Sausage and Wild Mushroom Stuffing

1 c. butter or margarine, softened	2 T. sesame oil
1 T. dried thyme, crushed	1/2 c. dry white wine
1 (14 to 16 lb.) turkey	1/4 c. all-purpose flour
1 T. salt	1 (16 oz.) ctn. half & half
1 T. pepper	1/2 tsp. soy sauce
Sausage & Wild Mushroom Stuffing (see below)	1/2 tsp. salt
2 T. soy sauce	1/2 tsp. pepper
	Fresh sage, for garnish

COMBINE butter and thyme, mixing well.

REMOVE giblets and neck from turkey; set aside.

RINSE turkey thoroughly with cold water and pat dry.

LOOSEN skin from breast without detaching it; carefully spread butter mixture under skin.

RUB outside of turkey evenly with 1 tablespoon salt and 1 tablespoon pepper.

SPOON 4 cups Sausage and Wild Mushroom Stuffing into turkey; truss turkey and tie ends of legs together with string.

LIFT wing tips up and over back, and tuck under bird.

PLACE turkey, breast-side up, in a large roasting pan; rub with 2 tablespoons soy sauce and oil.

BAKE at 375° for 2 1/2 hours, or until meat thermometer inserted into turkey thigh registers 180° and stuffing registers 165°, shielding turkey with aluminum foil after 1 hour and basting with pan juices every 30 minutes.

COOK giblets and neck in boiling water to cover, 45 minutes or until tender. Drain, reserving 1 cup broth. Coarsely chop neck meat and giblets; chill.

TRANSFER turkey to serving platter, reserving drippings in pan.

Continued on following page.

Meats

Continued from preceding page.

REMOVE and discard fat from drippings; pour 1/2 cup drippings into a heavy saucepan.

STIR wine and reserved broth into roasting pan, stirring to loosen particles.

PLACE 1/4 cup drippings over medium heat.

ADD flour and cook, whisking constantly, until browned.

GRADUALLY add wine mixture and half & half. Cook mixture, whisking constantly, until bubbly.

STIR in neck meat and giblets, 1/2 teaspoon soy sauce, salt and pepper. Simmer, stirring often, to desired thickness.

SERVE gravy with turkey.

GARNISH, if desired.

SAUSAGE AND WILD MUSHROOM STUFFING:

1/2 lb. ground pork sausage	1/2 tsp. pepper
1/2 c. butter or margarine	1 (14 1/2 oz.) can chicken broth
3 lb. mixed wild mushrooms (shiitake, portobello, enoki), sliced	1 (8 oz.) pkg. herb-seasoned stuffing mix
1 (14 1/2 oz.) can chicken broth	1 tsp. rosemary, thyme & sage
1/2 tsp. salt	1 lg. onion & 1 bunch green onions, sliced

BROWN sausage in large skillet, stirring to crumble. Drain and set aside.

MELT butter in skillet; add mushrooms, onion and green onions; sauté until tender.

STIR in sausage, broth and remaining ingredients. Spoon 4 cups stuffing into turkey or you may bake in lightly-greased 9x13-inch baking dish.

BAKE at 375° for 45 minutes or until lightly browned.

YIELD: 10 servings.

Smoked Turkey Casserole

A few years ago we received a smoked turkey as a gift, it was very delicious, but very difficult to find something to do with the leftovers. I found this one in Southern Living, and have used it several times. It is very good, and we like it with a crisp, crusty bread.

8 oz. uncooked penne	1/2 c. milk
6 oz. sliced ham, cut into 1/2" strips	1/4 tsp. pepper
6 oz. sliced smoked turkey, cut into 1/4" slices	8 tomato slices
	8 bacon slices, cooked
1 (10 3/4 oz.) can Cheddar cheese soup	1/4 c. refrigerated shredded Parmesan cheese

COOK pasta according to package directions; drain.
COMBINE pasta, ham and turkey in a bowl.
COMBINE soup, milk and pepper; stir into pasta mixture. Spoon into 4 lightly-greased individual baking dishes; top with tomato slices.
BAKE at 350° for 15 minutes. Top with bacon slices. Sprinkle with Parmesan cheese and bake 5 more minutes, or until casseroles are thoroughly heated. Serve immediately.
YIELD: 4 servings.

Spicy Turkey Pie

1/2 (10 oz.) pkg. frozen whole kernel corn
1/2 c. chicken broth
1/2 c. sliced celery
1 med. onion, cut into thin wedges
1/2 c. picante sauce
4 tsp. cornstarch
3 c. chopped, cooked turkey
1 (8 1/2 oz.) pkg. cornbread mix
1 1/2 c. shredded Cheddar cheese
2 (4 oz.) cans diced green chili peppers, drained

IN a saucepan, combine corn, broth, celery and onion.
BRING to boiling; reduce heat.
SIMMER, uncovered, 10 to 15 minutes.
ADD picante sauce.
STIR 2 tablespoons water into cornstarch; add to corn mixture.
COOK and stir until bubbly.
COOK 2 minutes more.
STIR in turkey.
POUR turkey mixture into 6x10x2-inch baking dish.
SPRINKLE with cheese and chili peppers.
SPOON cornbread on top.
BAKE at 425° for 20 minutes.

Standing Rib Roast with
Yorkshire Pudding

1 (4 lb.) beef rib roast
4 eggs
2 c. milk

2 c. all-purpose flour
3/4 tsp. salt

PLACE roast, fat-side up, in a 9x13-inch baking pan.

SEASON with salt and pepper.

INSERT a meat thermometer.

ROAST, uncovered, in a 325° oven for 2 1/2 to 3 1/4 hours, or until meat thermometer registers 140° for rare, 160° for medium, or 170° for well done.

REMOVE roast from pan.

COVER roast with foil; keep warm.

RESERVE 1/4 cup drippings.

INCREASE oven temperature to 400°.

IN a mixer bowl, beat eggs on low speed of an electric mixer for 1/2 minute.

ADD the milk; beat for 15 seconds.

ADD flour and salt; beat until combined, then beat for 2 minutes.

RETURN reserved drippings to baking pan.

POUR egg mixture into pan.

BAKE at 400° for 30 minutes; cut into squares.

SERVE with roast.

YIELD: 8 servings.

Stuffed Pork Chops
(With Apricots and Mushrooms)

4 T. butter or margarine,
    divided
1 (8 oz.) pkg. sliced fresh
    mushrooms
1/3 c. chopped onion
1/3 c. chopped celery
1 c. soft bread crumbs
1/2 c. dried apricots, chopped
1/2 c. chopped fresh parsley

1/2 tsp. rubbed sage
8 (1" thick) center-cut pork loin
    chops, cut with pockets*
2 tsp. salt
1 tsp. freshly-ground pepper
1 c. dry white wine
1 1/2 T. cornstarch
2 T. water

MELT 2 tablespoons butter in a large skillet over medium-high heat; add mushrooms, onion and celery. Cook, stirring constantly, 5 minutes or until tender. Stir in soft bread crumbs and the next 3 ingredients; remove from heat.

SPRINKLE both sides and pocket of each chop with salt and pepper. Spoon vegetable mixture evenly into pockets and secure with wooden toothpick.

MELT remaining 2 tablespoons butter in skillet. Add chops and cook until browned, turning once. Place chops in a lightly-greased roasting pan or shallow baking dish; add white wine.

BAKE, uncovered, at 350° for 45 minutes or until done. Remove chops from pan and discard wooden picks; keep chops warm.

REMOVE and discard fat from pan drippings. Place 1 1/2 cups drippings in a small saucepan.

COMBINE cornstarch and water, stirring constantly, until smooth. Stir into 1 1/2 cups drippings.

COOK over medium heat, stirring constantly, until mixture thickens and boils. Boil 1 minute, stirring constantly. Remove from heat; serve with chops.

YIELD: 8 servings.

*HAVE your butcher cut the pockets in your chops.

Sweet and Spicy Mustard Sauce or Dip

3 T. mayonnaise
3 T. coarse-grained Dijon
mustard

1 T. prepared horseradish
2 tsp. sugar

COMBINE all the ingredients in a glass bowl and microwave on HIGH 30 seconds, stirring once.
GREAT with chicken, chicken strips, etc.
YIELD: 1/3 cup.

Turkey Breast with Cranberry Salsa

1 (6 lb.) turkey breast
1 c. cranberry juice cocktail
1/4 c. orange juice
1/4 c. olive oil
1 tsp. salt
1 tsp. pepper
1/4 c. chopped fresh cilantro
3 c. frozen cranberries
1/2 c. honey
2 T. fresh lime juice

1/2 c. coarsely-chopped purple
onion
2 fresh jalapeño peppers, seeded
& coarsely chopped
1/2 c. coarsely-chopped dried
apricots
1/2 c. fresh cilantro leaves
2 lg. oranges, peeled, seeded &
coarsely chopped

REMOVE and discard skin and breast bone from turkey breast, separating breast halves. Place turkey in a large, heavy-duty, zip-top plastic bag.
COMBINE cranberry juice cocktail and the next 5 ingredients in a jar; cover marinade tightly, and shake vigorously. Reserve 1/2 cup marinade and place in refrigerator. Pour remaining marinade over turkey. Seal bag and refrigerate 8 hours, turning turkey occasionally.
POSITION knife blade in food processor bowl. Add frozen cranberries and the next 7 ingredients. Pulse until chopped, stopping once to scrape down sides (do not overprocess). Transfer cranberry mixture to a serving bowl; chill.
REMOVE turkey from marinade, discarding marinade.
COOK under broiler about 15 minutes on each side, or until a meat thermometer inserted into the thickest portion registers 170°, basting occasionally with reserved marinade. Let stand 10 minutes before slicing.
SERVE with cranberry mixture.
YIELD: 8 servings.

Meats

Turkey Crêpes

1/2 c. sliced, fresh mushrooms
1/3 c. chopped onion
1/3 c. chopped celery
Vegetable cooking spray
2 1/2 c. chopped, cooked
   turkey breast
1 (4 oz.) jar sliced pimento,
   drained

White Wine Sauce (recipe below)
Crêpes
1/3 c. grated Parmesan cheese
3/4 c. (3 oz.) shredded Cheddar
   cheese
1/3 c. slivered almonds, toasted
Garnishes: fresh parsley, cherry
   tomatoes

SAUTÉ the first 3 ingredients in a large skillet coated with cooking spray until vegetables are tender. Add turkey, pimento and 1 cup White Wine Sauce, stirring gently.

SPOON mixture down center of spotty-side of each crêpe, dividing mixture equally among crêpes. Fold sides over and place, seam-side up, in a lightly-greased 9x13x2-inch baking dish. Spoon remaining White Wine Sauce over crêpes.

COVER and bake at 350° for 20 minutes. Remove from oven; sprinkle with almonds. Garnish, if desired.

YIELD: 6 to 8 servings.

WHITE WINE SAUCE:
1/3 c. butter or margarine
1/3 c. all-purpose flour
1 1/2 c. half & half
1 1/4 c. milk

1/4 c. white wine
1 1/2 T. white wine
   Worcestershire sauce
1/2 tsp. salt
1/4 tsp. white pepper

MELT butter in a heavy saucepan over low heat. Add flour, stirring until smooth.

COOK 1 minute, stirring constantly. Gradually add half & half, milk and wine.

COOK over medium heat, stirring constantly, until thickened and bubbly.

Continued on following page.

Continued from preceding page.

STIR in Worcestershire sauce, salt and pepper.
REMOVE from heat.
YIELD: 3 cups.

CRÊPES:

2 eggs	1/4 tsp. salt
1 1/3 c. milk	1 1/2 T. vegetable oil
1 1/2 c. all-purpose flour	Vegetable cooking spray

COMBINE the first 5 ingredients in container of an electric blender; process 30 seconds. Scrape down sides of blender container with rubber spatula. Process an additional 30 seconds. Refrigerate batter 1 hour.
COAT bottom of a 6-inch crêpe pan or nonstick skillet with cooking spray; place over medium heat until just hot, not smoking. Pour 3 tablespoon batter into pan. Quickly tilt pan in all directions so batter covers pan in a thin film; cook 1 minute. Fill crêpe and cook about 30 seconds. Place crêpe on a towel to cool. Repeat until all batter is used. Stack between layers of waxed paper to prevent sticking.
YIELD: 12 (6-inch) crêpes.

Turkey Cutlets with Sage Gravy

5 (5 oz.) boneless turkey
    breast cutlets
1 tsp. dried whole-leaf sage,
    crumbled
2 T. butter

1/4 tsp. salt
1/8 tsp. pepper
1/8 tsp. paprika
1/2 c. all-purpose flour
2 T. olive oil

PLACE cutlets between sheets of heavy-duty plastic wrap; flatten to 1/4-inch thickness, using a meat mallet or rolling pin.
COMBINE sage, salt, pepper and paprika; rub evenly on each side of cutlets.
COVER.
REFRIGERATE 1 to 2 hours.
DREDGE cutlets in flour and shake off excess.
MELT butter in a large nonstick skillet over medium heat and add olive oil.
ADD cutlets and cook 3 minutes on each side, or until lightly browned.
TRANSFER cutlets to a serving plate and keep warm.
RESERVE drippings in skillet for Sage Gravy.
SERVE cutlets with Sage Gravy (see below).
YIELD: 4 servings.

SAGE GRAVY:
Reserved drippings
1/2 c. finely-chopped onion
1/2 c. finely-chopped carrot
1/4 c. finely-chopped celery
1 tsp. dried whole-leaf sage,
    crumbled
1/3 c. Chablis or other
    dry white wine

1/2 c. chicken broth
1 c. half & half
1/2 tsp. lemon juice
1/2 tsp. salt
1/2 tsp. pepper
2 T. cold water, cut in pieces

ADD onion and the next 3 ingredients to drippings in skillet.

Continued on following page.

Continued from preceding page.

COOK over medium heat, stirring constantly, until onion is tender.
ADD wine; bring to a boil and cook until liquid is reduced to about
2 tablespoons.
ADD broth and cook until liquid is reduced by half. Stir in half & half.
RETURN to a boil; cook until slightly thickened.
POUR mixture through a wire mesh strainer into a bowl; discard
vegetables.
RETURN mixture to skillet.
STIR in lemon juice, salt and pepper.
ADD butter pieces, 1 at a time, stirring with a wire whisk until
blended. (If butter is difficult to work into gravy, place a skillet over
low heat for a few seconds, being careful not to get mixture too hot.)
YIELD: 1 cup.

How to Thaw and Stuff a Turkey

To thaw a frozen turkey, place it in its original wrap on a tray; set it in the refrigerator and let the bird thaw. Depending on the size, allow 2 to 4 days for thawing.

A 4- to 12-pound turkey will take 1 to 2 days.
A 12- to 20-pound turkey will take 2 to 3 days.
A 20- to 24-pound turkey will take as long as 3 to 4 days.

Thawing in the refrigerator instead of at room temperature is the safest method to use, because it reduces the risk of bacterial growth.

Cold water thawing: Place turkey, breast-side down, in its unopened wrapper, in cold water to cover. Change water every 30 minutes to keep the surface cold. Estimate minimum thawing time to be 30 minutes per pound for whole turkey. Be sure to change water every 30 minutes so outside temperature of the bird does not rise too quickly and allow bacteria to grow.

After thawing the turkey, remove the wrappings and free legs and tail. Remove the giblets and neck piece tucked inside the bird. Rinse bird with cold running water and pat dry with paper towels. Season body cavity with salt, if desired. DO NOT stuff turkey until just before cooking. If you make your stuffing ahead of time, chill it separately.

Stuffing the turkey: Use 1/2 cup stuffing per pound for turkeys weighing up to 10 pounds. For turkeys weighing more than 10 pounds, use 3/4 cup stuffing per pound.

Spoon stuffing loosely into neck cavity; pull neck skin over stuffing and fasten securely to back of bird with a small skewer. Place turkey, neck-down, in a large mixing bowl. Lightly spoon more stuffing into the body cavity. Holding the turkey by its legs, gently shake the stuffing down. DO NOT PACK STUFFING or it will not heat through properly. It turkey has a band of skin across its tail, tuck drumsticks under band. Otherwise, tie legs securely to tail. Twist wing tips under back. For UNSTUFFED turkey, place quartered onions and celery in the body cavity.

Place extra stuffing in foil or casserole dish and cook alongside the turkey during the last hour of roasting, or until the stuffing's center is 160°.

Meats 117

How to Roast a Turkey

To roast a whole turkey, place thawed bird, breast up, on a rack in a shallow roasting pan. Make sure the rack holds the entire bird off the bottom of the pan. Brush the bird with cooking oil or melted butter or margarine. (There are many "specially seasoned" turkeys on the market, be sure to follow the directions on these turkeys very carefully, and if you have any questions call one of the turkey "hotlines".) To use a meat thermometer, insert it in the center thigh muscle, making sure the bulb does not touch bone.

Cover loosely with a foil "cap" that barely touches the turkey. Press lightly at ends of drumsticks and neck,

Place in a 325° oven. Baste dry areas occasionally with pan drippings, cooking oil or melted butter or margarine.

When turkey is 2/3 done, cut the band of skin or string between the legs so heat can reach inside thighs, it is not really necessary to keep the cavity tightly closed, as the heat needs to reach all of your turkey.

About 45 minutes before turkey is done, remove foil cap to assure even browning. Roast until thermometer registers 185°, or until the thickest part of drumstick is very soft and the whole drumstick moves up and down and twists easily in the socket.

Let the turkey rest for 15 minutes after you remove it from the oven. To keep the bird warm, cover it loosely with foil.

Carving the Turkey

Let the turkey stand at room temperature at least 15 minutes before carving. Make sure you have the proper carving utensils: you'll need a knife with a very sharp edge and a large two-tined carving fork. Carving may be done on a cutting board in the kitchen, or on the serving platter at the table.

Carve the bird with the breast-side up. Insert the carving fork to steady the turkey as you work. Cut the skin between the thigh and breast; bend the leg away from the bird to expose the leg joint. Slice through the joint and remove the leg.

Cut through the joint that separates the thigh and drumstick. Slice the dark meat from the bones of the leg and thigh rather than placing them whole on the serving platter.

The wing tips were twisted underneath the turkey before roasting, so you should be able to carve the turkey without removing them. You can slice them away at the shoulder joint, if necessary, to make carving easier.

To carve the breast, hold the bird securely with carving fork. Beginning at the meaty area above the shoulder joint, cut thin slices diagonally through the meat (across the grain), the entire length of the breast. Carve from one side of the turkey at a time, carving only as much meat as is needed to serve at a time.

Turkey Roasting Guide

Type	Ready-to-Cook Weight	Oven Temp.	# Will Serve	Guide to Roasting Time Unstuffed
	8 to 12 lb.	325°	2 to 4	2 3/4 to 3 hours
	12 to 14 lb.	325°	5 to 7	3 to 3 3/4 hours
Whole	14 to 18 lb.	325°	8 to 10	3 3/4 to 4 1/2 hours
	18 to 20 lb.	325°	11 to 13	4 1/4 to 4 1/2 hours
	20 to 24 lb.	325°	14 to 18	4 1/2 to 5 hours

Type	Ready-to-Cook Weight	Oven Temp.	# Will Serve	Guide to Roasting Time - Stuffed
Whole	8 to 12 lb.	325°	2 to 4	3 to 3 1/2 hours
	12 to 14 lb.	325°	5 to 7	3 1/2 to 4 hours
	14 to 18 lb.	325°	8 to 10	4 to 4 1/2 hours
	18 to 20 lb.	325°	10 to 12	4 1/4 to 4 3/4 hours
	20 to 24 lb.	325°	13 to 16	4 3/4 to 5 1/4 hours

Follow these guidelines or use a meat thermometer. Place thermometer in the thickest part of the thigh and roast until thermometer reads 185°.

Start checking for doneness about 30 minutes before recommended roasting times. Check the thickest part of the drumstick for softness, also when the whole drumstick moves up and down and twists easily in the socket.

The best rule for your stuffing, is to make in a separate baking dish. If you do stuff your turkey, remember the instructions of the previous page, and stuff it VERY loosely.

Freezing Your Leftover Turkey

Prefreezer Preparation:
REMOVE the stuffing from the bird and the meat from the bones as quickly as possible after serving. Wrap each separating and chill quickly.

CHOP, cube, grind or slice the meat, depending on how you plan to use it. Then divide the meat into meal-size portions and wrap them in moisture-vapor proof material. Seal, label and freeze. Do not refreeze cooked turkey that's been thawed.

IF you have a favorite casserole that calls for poultry, plan to make it with leftover turkey. You can save time by assembling the ingredients and freezing the unbaked mixture right in the ovenproof dish you will use for baking. Be sure to season these casseroles lightly before freezing. Then add additional seasoning during reheating.

Freezer Storage Time:
KEEP sliced turkey for sandwiches only 1 month. You can keep other forms of turkey for up to 6 months.

Thawing Instructions:
THAW leftover turkey meat in the refrigerator.

IF you are in a hurry, place the frozen meat in the microwave on DEFROST, taking care not to allow the meat to get too warm.

CASSEROLES need not be thawed. Place them directly in the oven. Bake, uncovered, in a 400° oven 1 to 2 hours. Casserole may be thawed in the refrigerator overnight, if desired. Cook as directed in the recipe, adding 15 to 20 minutes to the baking time.

NOTE: It is extremely important to take every precaution with dealing with preparation, cooking and storage of food products. Be sure to follow all steps necessary in every stage of food handling.

Meats

Notes &
Recipes

_____

_____

_____

_____

_____

_____

_____

_____

_____

_____

_____

_____

_____

_____

_____

_____

_____

_____

VEGETABLES

List Your Favorite Recipes

Recipes   **Page**

_____   _____

_____   _____

_____   _____

_____   _____

_____   _____

_____   _____

_____   _____

_____   _____

_____   _____

_____   _____

_____   _____

_____   _____

_____   _____

_____   _____

_____   _____

_____   _____

Apricot-Sweet Potato Bake

2 lb. sweet potatoes
(5 to 6 medium)
1 c. dried apricots, chopped
1/4 c. butter or margarine,
cut up

2 eggs
2 tsp. finely-shredded orange
peel
3/4 tsp. salt

IN a large saucepan, cook the sweet potatoes, covered, in enough boiling salted water to cover for 30 to 40 minutes, or until tender; drain and peel.

MEANWHILE, cook the apricots, covered, in boiling water for 10 minutes; drain.

IN a large mixer bowl, combine the sweet potatoes, apricots and butter; beat until fluffy.

ADD eggs, orange peel and salt; beat until combined.

TURN mixture into an ungreased 1 1/2-quart casserole.

BAKE, covered, in a 325° oven for 1 hour.

YIELD: 10 servings.

Artichoke-Spinach Casserole

1 (6 oz.) jar marinated
artichoke hearts, drained
2 (10 oz.) pkg. frozen
spinach, thawed
2 (3 oz.) pkg. cream cheese,
softened

2 T. butter, softened
4 T. milk
Freshly-ground black pepper,
1/2 c. freshly-grated Parmesan
cheese

PLACE artichokes in a 1 1/2-quart casserole.

SQUEEZE spinach dry and place on top of artichokes.

IN a small bowl, beat cream cheese and butter until smooth. Stir in milk.

SPREAD this mixture over the spinach; top with a grind of pepper and the Parmesan cheese.

COVER and refrigerate as long as 24 hours.

BAKE, covered, at 350° for 30 minutes, then uncover and bake 10 minutes.

YIELD: 6 to 8 servings.

Vegetables

123

Asparagus with Easy Orange Hollandaise

1 (10 oz.) pkg. frozen
    asparagus spears, or
    1 lb. asparagus
1/3 c. butter or margarine

1 T. frozen orange juice
    concentrate
2 egg yolks

COOK frozen asparagus according to package directions. (If using fresh asparagus, break off woody bases of asparagus at point where spears snap easily. Wash and scrape off scales. In a skillet or saucepan, cook, covered in a small amount of boiling salted water for 5 to 10 minutes, or until tender.)
COMBINE butter, orange juice concentrate and 1 tablespoon water; bring to boiling. Place egg yolks in blender container. Cover; blend until smooth.
WITH blender running on high speed, slowly add hot butter mixture through hole in lid; blend 30 seconds.
POUR over asparagus.
YIELD: 4 servings.

Baked Herb Spinach

1/2 stick margarine
1 c. finely-chopped onion
2 garlic cloves, minced
5 (10 oz.) pkg. frozen,
    chopped spinach, thawed
    & well drained
2 c. half & half (may use
    canned evaporated skim
    milk)

1 1/4 c. freshly-grated Parmesan
    cheese, divided
1/2 c. packaged bread crumbs,
    any flavor
1 tsp. crumbled dry marjoram
1 tsp. salt
1/4 tsp. freshly-ground black
    pepper

PREHEAT oven to 350°.
MELT margarine in a large skillet over medium-high heat.
ADD onion and garlic and sauté just until tender. Remove from heat and stir in spinach, half & half, 1 cup Parmesan cheese, bread crumbs, marjoram, salt and pepper.
POUR into a buttered, shallow 3-quart baking dish and sprinkle with remaining cheese.
BAKE 30 minutes, or until bubbly.
YIELD: 12 servings.

Baked Stuffed Potatoes

6 lg. yellow potatoes
Boiling water
1 c. cooked baby lima beans

4 T. butter or margarine
3 T. crumbs

WASH potatoes. Cook in a small amount of boiling water 20 minutes, or until nearly tender. Drain. Peel; slice tops off.

SCOOP out centers and save. Fill potatoes with lima beans. Dot with 3 tablespoons butter.

SPRAY 1 1/2-quart baking dish with nonstick vegetable spray. Place stuffed potatoes in prepared baking dish.

BAKE at 400° for 15 minutes, or longer, until tender.

SAUTÉ scooped-out potato centers with crumbs in remaining butter.

SPOON over potatoes.

CONTINUE to bake 5 minutes more, or until tops are browned.

Baked Sweet Potatoes with Melted Butter, Sour Cream and Brown Sugar

4 med. sweet potatoes
1 T. vegetable oil
2 T. butter or margarine,
 melted

1/2 c. sour cream
Salt & ground pepper, to taste
4 tsp. dark-brown sugar, or to
 taste

HEAT oven to 400°. Line a baking sheet with aluminum foil or parchment paper; set aside.

RUB the potatoes with vegetable oil and place on the prepared baking sheet.

BAKE in oven until potatoes can be easily pierced with a fork, 40 to 45 minutes. (You may roast the sweet potatoes on the BBQ grill, wrapped in heavy-duty foil.)

SLIT the potatoes lengthwise, and sprinkle with salt and pepper and melted butter.

TOP with a dollop of sour cream, sprinkle with the dark-brown sugar and serve.

YIELD: 4 servings.

Vegetables

Brandied Cranberries

3 (12 oz.) pkg. frozen or frozen   1/2 c. brandy
   (thawed) cranberries   Garnish: Fresh parsley (opt.)
3 c. sugar

PLACE cranberries in a single layer in 2 lightly-greased 10x15x1-inch jellyroll pans; pour sugar over cranberries and cover tightly with foil.
BAKE at 350° for 1 hour.
SPOON cranberries into a large serving bowl; gently stir in brandy. Cool.
SERVE chilled or at room temperature. Garnish, if desired.
STORE in refrigerator up to 1 week.
YIELD: 5 cups.

Brandied Sweet Potatoes

3 to 4 oranges, peeled   1/4 c. light cream (half & half)
1/4 c. firmly-packed brown   1/4 c. butter or margarine, melted
   sugar, + more for topping   1 tsp. salt
1 T. freshly-grated orange peel   4 c. cooked sweet potatoes or
1/2 c. brandy or Grand Marnier   yams
   (orange-flavored liqueur)

CUT 1 orange into thin slices and set aside. Cut remaining oranges into very small pieces to yield 2 cups drained fruit, and place in a large bowl.
SPRINKLE orange pieces with 1/4 cup brown sugar and set aside.
COMBINE grated peel, brandy, cream, butter and salt in a 1-quart saucepan over medium heat.
MEANWHILE place potatoes in a large mixing bowl and mash. When cream mixture is hot through, beat into potatoes until well blended.
STIR in drained, sweetened orange pieces, then spoon mixture into a greased 2-quart casserole; top with orange slices.
SPRINKLE lightly with additional brown sugar and bake, uncovered, 35 to 40 minutes. (Sometimes I sprinkle the top just at the last 10 minutes of baking with sugared pecans; do not have to be sugared.) You could also use miniature marshmallows, if desired.
YIELD: 8 servings.

NOTE: This casserole may be made well in advance and refrigerated until ready to bake. It is my VERY favorite, and I always make it ahead of time. It seems to have a richer flavor.

                                     Vegetables

Broccoli-Corn Bake

1 (16 oz.) can cream-style
    corn
1 (10 oz.) pkg. frozen
    chopped broccoli,
    cooked & drained
1 beaten egg
1/2 c. coarse saltine
    cracker crumbs

1 T. instant minced onion
2 T. margarine, melted
1/2 tsp. salt
Pepper
1/4 c. coarse saltine cracker
    crumbs
1 T. margarine, melted

COMBINE the corn, broccoli, egg, the 1/2 cup cracker crumbs, onion,
2 tablespoons melted margarine, salt and pepper; turn into a 1-quart
casserole.
COMBINE the 1/4 cup cracker crumbs and the remaining margarine;
sprinkle over the vegetable mixture.
BAKE, uncovered, in a 350° oven for 35 to 40 minutes.
YIELD: 6 servings.

Vegetables

Carrot Mousse Tart

4 lg. carrots, very thinly
   sliced
1 T. butter or margarine,
   melted
3 c. shredded carrots (about
   8 medium-size carrots)
1 potato, peeled & cubed

1/4 c. sour cream
1 tsp. finely-shredded orange
   peel
1/4 tsp. salt
1/8 tsp. ground turmeric (opt.)
1/8 tsp. ground white pepper

IN a saucepan cook sliced carrots in a small amount of boiling salted water for 3 to 4 minutes, or until crisp-tender; drain.

BRUSH an 8-inch round flan or cake pan with butter, or use nonstick spray.

BEGINNING in the center of the pan and working toward the outer edges, arrange the drained carrot slices in circles, petal fashion, slightly overlapping and pressing them onto sides of pan; set aside.

FILLING: Cook shredded carrots and potato into a small amount of boiling salted water about 15 minutes, or just until tender; drain well.

IN food processor bowl or blender container, place the eggs, sour cream, orange peel, salt, turmeric, if desired, and pepper. Add half of the cooked carrots and potato.

COVER and blend until nearly smooth. Turn into the carrot-lined pan; smooth top.

BAKE at 350° for 30 to 35 minutes, or until set; let stand 5 minutes.

WITH a knife, carefully loosen carrot slices from sides of pan.

PLACE a serving tray or plate atop pan; invert mousse, carefully lifting pan off. (You may have to replace any carrot slices remaining in pan.)

CUT into wedges and serve hot.

YIELD: 8 servings.

Corn Pudding

2 c. corn, cream-style or whole, or half of each	3 T. melted butter
2 T. minced onion	1 T. sugar
1 tsp. salt	2 c. milk
Pinch of salt (1/8 tsp.)	2 beaten eggs
	1 c. crushed saltines

MIX together corn and crackers; add onion, salt, melted butter and sugar.

BEAT eggs; add milk and combine with corn mixture.

POUR into greased (or sprayed with nonstick cooking spray) casserole.

BAKE at 350° for about 30 minutes, or until firm.

Cranberry Sweet Potatoes

3 lg. sweet potatoes	2 T. margarine or butter
1/2 c. cranberry-orange relish	1/4 c. packed brown sugar
1/4 c. raisins	1/4 c. broken walnuts

COOK sweet potatoes in boiling salted water for 25 to 35 minutes, or until tender. Cut in half lengthwise. Scoop out centers, leaving 1/4-inch-thick shells; set aside.

MASH centers; add relish. Beat until fluffy. Stir in raisins. Spoon into shells.

PLACE into a 7 1/2 x 12 x 2-inch baking dish that has been sprayed with nonstick vegetable spray.

CUT butter into brown sugar; stir in nuts. Sprinkle over sweet potatoes.

BAKE at 350° for 30 minutes.

YIELD: 6 servings.

Vegetables

Do-Ahead Mashed Potatoes

These potatoes are great for the holidays.

4 to 5 lg. all-purpose potatoes,   Milk or cream
    peeled & cooked   Butter or margarine
Salt, to taste

MASH cooked potatoes and season with salt; add milk and butter to reach the desired consistency. (You may want to decrease or omit the butter that goes into the potato mixture, because more will go on top). BUTTER (or use nonstick vegetable spray) a 2-quart casserole and spoon mashed potatoes into it. Melt enough butter or margarine to cover the surface of the potatoes completely.
SMOOTH the surface so that it is completely sealed with melted butter. Cool slightly, then refrigerate, covered.
BEFORE serving, preheat oven to 300°; poke some holes through the butter and potatoes so butter trickles down into potatoes.
BAKE until heated through.
YIELD: 6 to 10 servings.

Eggplant Casserole

1 med. to lg. eggplant, peeled & diced	1 sm. green pepper, chopped
Salt, to taste	1 T. brown sugar
1/2 c. margarine, divided	2 T. flour
1 sm. onion, chopped	1 (1 lb.) can tomatoes, cut up, with liquid
1 c. cornbread or jalapeño cornbread crumbs	Grated yellow cheese (Cheddar)

PLACE eggplant in a large saucepan; add 1/2 teaspoon salt and a small amount of water.

PLACE over medium heat and cook until tender, 8 to 10 minutes; drain well.

MELT half the margarine in a saucepan and add onion and bell pepper; sauté until onion is translucent.

ADD remaining margarine and melt. Stir in sugar, 1 teaspoon salt and flour.

COOK, stirring to blend.

ADD tomatoes and simmer 5 minutes, stirring.

STIR in cornbread crumbs and eggplant.

POUR into greased 1 1/2-quart casserole and bake 15 minutes.

TOP with cheese and bake at 350° for 10 to 15 minutes, or until cheese has melted.

YIELD: 4 to 6 servings.

Fried Corn and Onions

1/3 c. butter or margarine	2 (12 oz.) cans Mexican-style whole kernel corn, drained
2 med. onions, thinly sliced	

MELT butter in skillet; add onion and sprinkle with salt and a dash of pepper.

COVER; cook over low heat 5 minutes, shaking skillet often.

ADD corn; mix well.

HEAT, uncovered, 5 minutes; stir often.

SEASON to taste. Garnish with sprigs of parsley.

YIELD: 6 to 8 servings.

NOTE: This makes a very festive holiday vegetable, and is very quick and easy to prepare.

Garlic Mashed Potatoes

5 to 6 lg. potatoes, such as russets	1/2 c. milk or half & half, or more as needed
1 tsp. salt, divided	Freshly-ground white or black
3 T. butter	pepper, to taste
Roasted garlic (see note)	

PEEL potatoes and cut into chunks. Place in a medium-size saucepan and add enough water to cover potatoes. Add 1/2 teaspoon salt.
PLACE pot over high heat and bring to a boil. When water boils, cover pot.
TURN heat down to medium and cook potatoes, covered, 12 minutes.
WHEN potatoes are done, turn off the burner and drain potatoes in a colander.
RETURN potatoes to the pan; place the pan, uncovered, on the turned-off burner for a few seconds to help the potatoes dry out.
REMOVE the pan from the burner, and mash potatoes or whip with a portable electric mixer, directly in pan. When smooth, add butter, milk, remaining salt and pepper; mash or whip again, until as smooth as desired.
WHEN roasted garlic is cool enough to handle, squeeze garlic cloves out of their skins; discard skins.
MIX the soft, cooked garlic pulp into the mashed potatoes.
YIELD: 4 servings.

NOTE: I increase this recipe according to the size of the crowd I am serving.
NOTE: To roast garlic, wrap a whole head of garlic in foil. Place garlic on baking sheet and bake in a 400° oven until soft, 30 minutes to 1 hour. Use as directed in recipe above.

Harvard Beets

1/2 c. sugar	2 c. cooked or canned beets,
1/2 T. cornstarch	sliced or cubed
1/4 c. mild vinegar	2 T. butter
1/4 c. water	

MIX the sugar and cornstarch; add the vinegar and water; boil together 5 minutes.
ADD the beets and let stand at least 30 minutes, away from heat.
JUST before serving, bring to the boiling point and add the butter.
YIELD: 4 to 6 servings.

Vegetables

Lemon-Butter Potatoes

3 lb. sm. red potatoes	1 tsp. salt
1 med. size onion, sliced	Boiling water
3 slices lemon	1/4 c. margarine, melted
1 T. fresh lemon juice	

WASH unpeeled potatoes; put in 3-quart saucepan with onion, lemon slices and salt.

COVER with boiling water and cook over medium-high heat until tender; drain.

IN a small saucepan over medium-low heat, whisk together margarine and lemon juice.

WHEN ready to serve, remove lemon slices from potatoes and pour hot lemon butter sauce over potatoes.

YIELD: 6 servings.

Nutmeg Squash

3 1/2 to 4 lb. winter squash (butternut, acorn or hubbard), cut in lg. pieces	1/2 tsp. salt
	1/2 tsp. ground nutmeg
	Brown sugar (opt.)
2 T. butter or margarine	Poached apple wedges (opt.)
2 T. brown sugar	

PLACE squash pieces in a large saucepan or Dutch oven. Cook squash in a small amount of boiling salted water, covered, for 20 to 25 minutes or until tender; drain.

SCOOP pulp from rind of the squash. Mash the pulp (if your squash seems too thin, place in a saucepan. Cook, uncovered, until squash is desired consistency.)

STIR in butter or margarine, the brown sugar, salt and nutmeg. Heat through.

TRANSFER the squash mixture to a serving bowl. Sprinkle with additional brown sugar, if desired. Garnish the squash with poached apple wedges, if desired.

YIELD: 8 servings.

Vegetables

Orange Mashed Potatoes

1/4 c. butter or margarine	3/4 c. orange juice
2 c. finely-chopped onion	1 tsp. salt
3 lb. baking potatoes	Garnish: orange zest
1/2 c. sour cream	

MELT butter in a large skillet over medium-high heat; add onion and cook, stirring constantly, until browned. Set aside.
PEEL potatoes; cut into fourths.
COOK potatoes in boiling water to cover 15 minutes, or until potatoes are tender; drain.
BEAT potatoes, sour cream and orange juice at medium speed with an electric mixer until mixture is fluffy. Stir in onion and salt.
GARNISH, if desired.
YIELD: 8 servings.

Pea and Potato Casserole

1 (10 oz.) pkg. frozen peas	1 (12 oz.) pkg. frozen shredded
1 (10 3/4 oz.) can condensed	hash brown potatoes, thawed
cream of chicken soup	1 (8 1/4 oz.) can sliced carrots,
1/2 c. milk	drained
1/4 c. mayonnaise or salad	1/2 c. shredded American cheese
dressing	(2 oz.)
1 tsp. dried dill weed	

RUN hot water over frozen peas in a colander until separated; set aside.
IN a small mixing bowl stir together soup, milk, mayonnaise and dill weed.
ARRANGE half of the potatoes in a 6x10x2-inch baking dish that has been sprayed with nonstick spray.
TOP with half of the peas, then all of the sliced carrots. Spread half the soup mixture on top. Repeat with remaining potatoes, peas and soup mixture.
BAKE, uncovered, in a 350° oven for 30 minutes.
SPRINKLE cheese on top and bake, uncovered, for 5 additional minutes.
YIELD: 8 to 10 servings.

Potatoes Supreme

Nonstick spray coating	1 egg
6 med. potatoes	1 T. grated Parmesan cheese
4 oz. cream cheese	1 T. fine, dry bread crumbs
1 tsp. chopped green onion	1/2 tsp. chives (opt.)
1/4 tsp. salt	2 tsp. margarine or butter, melted
1/3 c. milk	1/8 tsp. pepper

SPRAY 6 individual soufflé dishes with nonstick spray coating. Set aside.
PEEL and cut up potatoes. Cook, covered, in boiling salted water for
10 to 15 minutes, or until tender; drain.
MASH with an electric mixer on low speed; add cream cheese, salt,
and a dash of pepper.
GRADUALLY beat in enough of the milk to make potato mixture
light and fluffy. Beat in egg.
SPOON potato mixture into a pastry bag fitted with large star tip; pipe
into dishes. (You may simply spoon potato mixture into dishes,
mounding on the top.)
IN a small dish, combine Parmesan cheese, dry bread crumbs and
margarine; sprinkle over potatoes.
BAKE at 325° for 25 to 30 minutes (30 to 35 minutes for chilled
dishes), or until heated through.
YIELD: 6 servings.

NOTE: This dish may be made the day before and refrigerated until
ready to bake. This can really help when getting ready for a big meal.

Quick Cranberry Relish

1 (16 oz.) can whole cranberry sauce	1/4 tsp. ground cinnamon
	1/8 tsp. ground cloves
1/2 c. chopped walnuts	Chopped walnuts (opt.)
1/2 c. light raisins	

IN a small mixing bowl, stir together cranberry sauce, the 1/2 cup
chopped walnuts, raisins, cinnamon and cloves.
COVER and chill cranberry mixture thoroughly in the refrigerator.
STIR relish, and sprinkle additional chopped walnuts over relish
before serving, if desired.
YIELD: 12 servings.

Vegetables

Sautéed Portobello Mushrooms

3 lb. fresh portobello mush-
    rooms, may substitute
    fresh, see below*
12 garlic cloves, minced

2/3 c. olive oil
3/4 c. fresh parsley, chopped
1/4 tsp. salt
1/8 tsp. pepper

CUT mushrooms into 1/4-inch slices (*if using fresh mushrooms, do not slice; stir constantly during cooking.)
SAUTÉ half of garlic in half of oil in an electric skillet or extra-large skillet over medium heat until tender.
ADD half the mushrooms and 1/4 cup parsley; cook 3 to 5 minutes, or until tender and browned, turning once.
REMOVE to a serving dish; sprinkle with half of salt and pepper.
REPEAT procedure; sprinkle with remaining 1/4 cup parsley. Serve immediately.
YIELD: 12 servings.

Sour Cream Green Beans

1 (16 oz.) pkg. frozen cut
    green beans
1 sm. onion, chopped
1 T. butter or margarine
1/2 tsp. salt

1 T. all-purpose flour
1/4 tsp. dried dill weed
1/2 c. chicken broth
1/2 c. dairy sour cream
1/2 tsp. pepper

COOK the green beans according to package directions; drain well.
IN a large saucepan, cook onion in butter until tender, but not brown.
STIR in flour, dill weed, salt and pepper. Add chicken broth all at once.
COOK and stir until thickened and bubbly; cook and stir for 1 minute more.
REMOVE from heat; stir in sour cream.
ADD green beans to sour cream mixture. Heat through, but do not boil.
TURN mixture into a heated serving bowl.
YIELD: 8 servings.

Vegetables

Stuffed Sweet Potatoes

6 med. to lg. sweet potatoes	1/4 tsp. salt
or yams (6 to 8 oz. each)	1/2 tsp. ground cinnamon
2 T. margarine or butter	1/4 tsp. ground nutmeg
1/4 c. orange marmalade	1/4 c. finely-chopped walnuts

SCRUB potatoes; prick with a fork. Bake in a 425° oven for 40 to 60 minutes, or until tender.

CUT a lengthwise slice from the top of each potato; remove skin from slices and put the pulp into a medium mixing bowl. Scoop out each potato, leaving a 1/4-inch shell. Add the pulp to mixing bowl.

MASH potatoes; add margarine, marmalade, salt, cinnamon and nutmeg. Mash until well blended.

SPOON mixture into potato shells. Sprinkle chopped nuts on top.

PLACE in 7 1/2 x 12 x 2-inch baking dish, that has been sprayed with nonstick vegetable spray.

BAKE, uncovered, in a 425° oven for 10 to 15 minutes, or until heated through.

NOTE: These potatoes may be made the day before and refrigerated for up to 24 hours. Bake, covered, in a 425° oven for 30 to 35 minutes, or until heated through.

Vegetables

Tangy Pasta Nests and Vegetables

2 c. frozen loose-pack
cauliflower, broccoli &
carrots
6 oz. fettuccine
3 T. butter or margarine
2 T. all-purpose flour

Salt & pepper, to taste
1 tsp. grated lemon peel
3/4 c. milk
1 c. dairy sour cream
1 beaten egg
1/4 c. grated Parmesan cheese

IN separate pans, cook vegetables and pasta according to package directions; drain.

CUT up any large vegetable pieces.

IN a saucepan melt butter, stir in flour, peel, salt and pepper; stir in milk. Cook and stir until thickened and bubbly.

STIR in sour cream and vegetables. Heat almost to boiling.

SPOON half of the sauce into a 7 1/2 x 12 x 2-inch baking dish sprayed with nonstick coating.

TOSS together cooked pasta, egg and Parmesan cheese. Using a long-tined fork, twirl a few strands of the fettuccine around tines. Remove the pasta from the fork, standing pasta upright in baking dish to form a nest.

CONTINUE forming nests in baking dish to make 6 portions with 3 nests each.

SPOON remaining vegetable sauce over pasta.

COVER and bake at 350° for about 20 minutes, or until heated through.

YIELD: 6 servings.

Three-Bean Bake

1/2 c. butter or margarine	1 (No. 2) can green lima beans
1/2 c. minced, peeled onions	1 (1 lb.) can Boston-style baked
1 clove garlic, peeled and sliced	beans
3/4 c. brown sugar	1 c. ketchup
1 tsp. dry mustard	2 T. vinegar
2 (No. 2) cans kidney beans,	Salt & pepper
drained	1/2 c. molasses

HEAT butter or margarine in skillet. Sauté onions and garlic together 5 minutes, or until onions are tender.

STIR in brown sugar, mustard, kidney beans, limas and baked beans, ketchup and vinegar. Mix well. Taste for seasoning. Add salt and pepper as needed.

POUR into 2-quart casserole that has been sprayed with nonstick vegetable spray.

BAKE, covered, at 350° for 25 minutes. Uncover and bake 5 minutes more, or until mixture has thickened and baked together.

YIELD: 8 servings.

Wild Rice and Mushrooms

1 (3 oz.) can broiled sliced	1 c. long-grain rice
mushrooms	2 T. butter or margarine
1 can condensed beef broth	2 T. snipped parsley, or 1 T.
2 med. onions, finely chopped	dried parsley
1/2 c. wild rice	

DRAIN mushrooms, reserving liquid.

COMBINE mushroom liquid and beef broth; add water to make 2 cups.

IN a saucepan, bring broth mixture and onions to boiling. Add washed wild rice; reduce heat; cover and simmer 20 minutes.

ADD long-grain rice; return to boiling, then reduce heat, cover and simmer 20 minutes longer, or until rice is done.

ADD mushrooms and butter; heat briefly, then add parsley.

YIELD: 6 to 8 servings.

Vegetables

Zesty Carrots

6 to 8 carrots, cooked & cut into strips	1/2 tsp. salt
1/4 c. water or cooking liquid from carrots	1/4 tsp. freshly-ground pepper
2 T. grated onion	1/4 c. saltine cracker crumbs
2 T. prepared horseradish	1 T. butter, softened
1/2 c. mayonnaise (Hellmann's)	Dash of paprika
	Chopped parsley for garnish (opt.)

ARRANGE carrot strips in a shallow dish.
IN a small bowl, combine water, onion, horseradish, mayonnaise, salt and pepper, then pour over carrots.
TOP with a mixture of cracker crumbs, butter and paprika.
BAKE in a 375° oven for 15 to 20 minutes. Garnish.
YIELD: 6 servings.

PUNCHES AND DRINKS

List Your Favorite Recipes

Recipes   **Page**

_____   _____

_____   _____

_____   _____

_____   _____

_____   _____

_____   _____

_____   _____

_____   _____

_____   _____

_____   _____

_____   _____

_____   _____

_____   _____

_____   _____

_____   _____

_____   _____

_____   _____

_____   _____

Cardinal Punch

1 1/2 c. boiling water
2 T. black tea
1/4 tsp. ground allspice
1/4 tsp. ground cinnamon
1/8 tsp. nutmeg
3/4 c. sugar

1 (1 pt.) btl. cranberry
   juice cocktail
1/2 c. orange juice
1/3 c. lemon juice
1 1/2 c. cold water

POUR the rapidly boiling water over tea; add spices.
COVER and let steep 5 minutes.
STRAIN and stir in sugar.
ADD cranberry, orange and lemon juices, and cold water.
COVER; chill thoroughly.
YIELD: 8 servings.

Champagne Punch

6 oranges, unpeeled &
   thinly sliced
1 c. sugar

2 bottles dry white wine
3 bottles sparkling wine,
   chilled

PLACE orange slices in a large nonmetallic container, and sprinkle
with sugar.
ADD white wine; cover and chill at least 8 hours.
STIR in sparkling white wine.
YIELD: 1 gallon.

Christmas Cranberry Drinks

BASIC CRANBERRY SYRUP:

3 lb. whole cranberries   5 c. sugar
2 qt. water   5 sticks cinnamon

COMBINE ingredients in a large kettle; bring to a boil.
MASH cranberries with potato masher; simmer 15 minutes.
STRAIN through several layers of cheesecloth.
STIR in enough water to make 2 1/2 quarts syrup.
STORE in refrigerator.
SERVE iced or very cold, mixed with other fruit juices, ginger ale or iced tea, as desired.

VARIATIONS:

Cranberry/Apple Drink: Mix equal portions of Basic Cranberry Syrup, apple juice and tonic water.

Cranberry Cooler: Mix 1 part Basic Cranberry Syrup with 2 parts chilled ginger ale.

Cranberry/Lemon Sparkle: Combine 2 (6-ounce) cans frozen lemonade concentrate and 1 quart Basic Cranberry Syrup. Add 1 1/2 quarts water and 1 1/2 quarts ginger ale. Yield: 18 cups.

Cranberry Tea: Mix equal portions of Basic Cranberry Syrup, tonic water and iced tea.

Christmas Raspberry Punch

3 qt. raspberry sherbet   5 qt. chilled ginger ale

PLACE large chunks of raspberry sherbet in punch bowl.
POUR ginger ale over, holding bottles some little distance above the punch bowl.
GARNISH with fresh mint leaves and maraschino cherries, if desired.
YIELD: 55 punch-cup servings.

THIS makes a very festive punch.

Cooked Custard Eggnog

1 qt. milk	1/4 tsp. ground nutmeg
6 eggs	1 tsp. vanilla extract
Dash of salt	1 c. whipping cream, whipped
1/2 c. sugar	Ground nutmeg

HEAT milk in a large saucepan (do not boil).

BEAT eggs and salt in a large bowl; gradually add sugar, mixing well.
Gradually stir about 1/4 of hot milk into egg mixture; add to remaining hot milk, stirring constantly.

COOK over medium-low heat, stirring constantly, until mixture thickens and reaches 160°.

STIR in 1/4 teaspoon nutmeg and vanilla.

SET saucepan in large pan of ice for 10 minutes to rapidly cool mixture.

COVER and refrigerate up to 48 hours.

WHEN ready to serve, fold in whipped cream and sprinkle with ground nutmeg.

YIELD: 7 cups.

Cranberry-Lemonade Punch

1 quart cranberry juice cocktail	1 qt. ginger ale, chilled
1 qt. pink lemonade	1 qt. raspberry sherbet or sorbet
1 qt. orange juice	

COMBINE the first 4 ingredients in a large bowl; chill.

STIR in ginger ale; scoop sherbet into punch.

SERVE immediately.

YIELD: 1 1/2 gallons.

Cranberry Wassail

1 (32 oz.) btl. Ocean Spray
    Cranberry Juice Cocktail
1 1/4 c. apple juice
3 T. sugar
1 (3") cinnamon stick

1/2 tsp. whole allspice
2 slices orange, for garnish
4 whole cloves, for garnish
1/2 c. brandy (opt.)

COMBINE all ingredients, except garnishes and brandy, in a large saucepan; heat to boiling, reduce heat and simmer 10 minutes.
STRAIN punch to remove spices.
PLACE In a heatproof punch bowl; stir in brandy, if desired.
GARNISH with orange slices studded with cloves.
YIELD: 10 (4-ounce) servings.

Easy Eggnog

2 pt. vanilla ice cream,
    softened

1/2 to 3/4 c. bourbon
1 qt. commercial eggnog

JUST before serving, spoon heaping tablespoons of ice cream into punch bowl.
POUR eggnog over ice cream; and bourbon to taste, and stir gently.
YIELD: 2 quarts.

Eggnog

1 doz. eggs
1 c. sugar, may need a little
    more
1 1/2 qt. milk

1 pt. heavy cream, whipped
1 btl. (3 1/8 c.) cognac
Powdered cinnamon or nutmeg

SEPARATE eggs. Beat yolks until light, in large bowl in which the nog is to be served. Add sugar while still beating.
STIR in milk and cream.
POUR cognac into this mixture very slowly, stirring to mix. Taste for sweetness; add more sugar if needed.
COVER and let stand in refrigerator 1 or 2 hours.
JUST before serving, beat egg whites until stiff. Gently mix in with the nog.
DUST cinnamon or nutmeg over the top and serve.
YIELD: 20 or more servings.

Flaming Coffee Brulot

1 c. brandy	2 (1") cinnamon sticks
1/4 c. sugar	10 whole cloves
6 (2") strips orange & lemon peel	4 c. hot, strong, black coffee

COMBINE ingredients in a medium saucepan; heat gently until warmed.

SET aflame with match, taking special care with fire; allow flame to burn 1 minute, then slowly stir in the black coffee. Serve at once. YIELD: 5 cups.

Ginger Claret Punch

1 c. sugar	2 (1") strips lemon peel
1 c. water	2 (1") strips orange peel
1/2 tsp. nutmeg	3 c. claret or Burgundy wine
1/2 tsp. ginger	2 c. ginger ale, chilled
1 (2") piece stick cinnamon	Thin orange slices
6 whole cloves	Thin lemon slices

IN a medium saucepan, combine sugar, water, nutmeg, ginger, cinnamon, and the lemon and orange peels, with the 6 cloves pushed into them.

BRING to a boil, stirring to dissolve sugar.

REDUCE heat and simmer, uncovered, 5 minutes.

REMOVE from heat, cover and let stand until cool.

WITH slotted spoon, remove cinnamon stick and clove-stuffed lemon and orange peel.

ADD 3 cups claret or Burgundy wine; chill.

WHEN ready to serve, add 2 cups ginger ale, chilled, and garnish with thin orange and lemon slices.

YIELD: 6 cups.

*NOTE: TO serve hot, omit ginger ale and add wine to hot, spiced syrup. Bring again to a simmer and serve hot. Yield will be reduced to 4 cups.

Hot Apple Punch

2 1/4 c. sugar
4 c. water
2 (2 1/2") sticks cinnamon
8 whole allspice berries
10 whole cloves

1 whole piece ginger root
   (about the size of a quarter)
4 c. orange juice
2 c. lemon juice
2 qt. apple cider or juice

COMBINE sugar and water and boil 5 minutes.
REMOVE from heat; add spices. Let beverage stand, covered, 1 hour.
STRAIN.
JUST before serving, combine syrup, fruit juices and cider; bring
quickly to boiling. Remove from heat; serve at once.
YIELD: 4 1/2 quarts.

Hot Cranberry Punch

2 c. water
1 1/2 to 2 c. sugar
4 cinnamon sticks
36 whole cloves
2 qt. cranberry juice
   cocktail

1 qt. orange juice
1 1/2 to 2 c. lemon juice
1 lemon, sliced
1 orange, sliced
1 c. rum or 2 T. rum flavoring

COMBINE the first 4 ingredients in a large Dutch oven; bring to a boil
over high heat.
REDUCE heat and simmer 7 minutes.
REMOVE and discard spices.
ADD cranberry juice cocktail and remaining ingredients, and cook
over medium heat until thoroughly heated.
YIELD: about 5 quarts.

Punches and Drinks

Hot Mulled Cider

6 c. apple cider	1/2 tsp. ginger
1/2 c. light brown sugar	12 whole cloves
1 (2") piece stick cinnamon	2 oranges, sliced
1 tsp. nutmeg	2 lemons, sliced

IN a large saucepan, combine 6 cups apple cider, light brown sugar, stick cinnamon, nutmeg and ginger.

PUSH the whole cloves into the rinds of the sliced oranges and lemons, using 2 cloves per slice.

BRING mixture to a boil, stirring only to dissolve sugar.

REDUCE heat, cover and simmer 5 minutes.

YIELD: 6 cups.

Mulled Apricot Nectar

1 (46 oz.) can apricot nectar	15 whole cloves
1/2 lemon, sliced	8 whole allspice berries
2 (2 1/2") sticks cinnamon	

COMBINE all ingredients in heavy saucepan and bring to boiling point; simmer gently 5 minutes.

REMOVE from heat; cover; allow to stand 30 minutes.

STRAIN. If you wish, sweeten to taste with honey or sugar.

HEAT before serving.

YIELD: 5 cups.

Old English Syllabub

This is a recipe from an old, old recipe book I found of my mother's. It is very thick and needs to be sipped through a straw or eaten with a spoon. The recipe has been adapted to modern appliances.

3 eggs, separated	1/2 c. lemon juice
1 c. sugar	2 c. heavy cream, whipped

IN a blender, blend egg yolks until thick.
WHILE still blending, add 3/4 cup sugar and lemon juice.
IN a medium bowl, beat egg whites until frothy, gradually adding the remaining sugar.
BEAT until thick and glossy.
FOLD in egg yolk mixture and the 2 cups of cream, whipped.
BLEND all together very gently.
YIELD: 6 cups.

Rum and Coffee Cream

1 qt. coffee ice cream	1/2 c. rum or brandy

PLACE ice cream and rum or brandy in a blender or food processor; cover and blend until smooth.
FREEZE.

RUM CAFE AU LAIT:

6 c. hot strong coffee	4 to 6 cinnamon sticks
1/2 c. Rum & Coffee Cream	

FOR each serving, pour coffee into mugs; top with a scoop of the cream mixture.
INSERT a cinnamon stick as a stirrer.

Punches and Drinks

Spicy Perked Punch

2 qt. cranberry juice
    cocktail
1 qt. pineapple juice
1 qt. water
2/3 c. brown sugar, firmly packed

1 T. whole cloves
1 T. whole allspice
4 (2") sticks cinnamon
2 lemons, sliced & quartered

COMBINE fruit juices and water in a 30-cup electric percolator.
PLACE remaining ingredients in basket.
PERCOLATE about 30 minutes; serve from percolator.
YIELD: 5 quarts or 28 servings.

Tea Punch

2/3 c. boiling water
2 reg.-size tea bags
1 1/2 c. pineapple juice
1 c. grapefruit juice
1 c. orange juice

1/2 c. lemon juice
1 1/4 c. sugar
4 c. ginger ale, chilled
2 c. ice water

POUR boiling water over tea bags; cover and let stand 5 minutes.
REMOVE and discard tea bags.
COMBINE tea and fruit juices in a large pitcher or bowl; add sugar, stirring until it dissolves.
CHILL.
STIR in ginger ale and ice water, and serve immediately.
YIELD: 2 1/2 quarts.

Wine Spritzer

2 c. tawny port wine
1 c. club soda, chilled
6 thin orange slices

6 thin lemon slices
1 lime, cut into 6 wedges

IN a 1-quart pitcher, combine 2 cups port and 1 cup club soda, chilled.
POUR immediately over ice in 6 tall glasses, into which 1 slice each of orange and lemon has been placed.
GARNISH each with a wedge of lime.
YIELD: 3 cups.

Notes &
Recipes

_____
_____
_____
_____
_____
_____
_____
_____
_____
_____
_____
_____
_____
_____
_____
_____
_____

DESSERTS

List Your Favorite Recipes

Recipes   **Page**

Almond Torte Cake

1 c. almonds, sliced or flaked	1 c. soft shortening
3 c. sifted all-purpose flour	2/3 c. evaporated milk
2 c. sugar	1/2 c. water
4 tsp. baking powder	1 T. vanilla
1 tsp. salt	4 eggs, unbeaten

GREASE two (9x2-inch) round cake pans well, and flour bottom and sides of pans.

SPRINKLE sliced almonds over bottom of pans, 1/2 cup per pan.

SIFT flour, sugar, baking powder and salt into a 3-quart bowl.

ADD shortening, evaporated milk, water and vanilla, and beat 2 minutes with mixer at medium speed.

ADD eggs and continue to beat 1 minute more.

POUR batter over sliced almonds.

BAKE at 350° for 45 minutes, or until cake springs back when touched lightly.

CARAMEL FROSTING:

1/3 c. sift butter	1/2 c. brown sugar
2 tsp. vanilla	1/4 c. evaporated milk
2 to 3 drops almond extract	3 1/2 c. sifted powdered sugar

MIX butter, vanilla and almond extract well in a 1 1/2-quart bowl.

BEAT brown sugar in gradually with electric mixer, about 1/3 cup at a time, until smooth.

IF the frosting is too thick when you go to ice cake, add a few more drops of evaporated milk.

FROST between cake layers and on sides of cake, frosting only a very little around top of cake, leaving almonds on top of cake unfrosted.

Apricot Mousse

20 ladyfingers
3 (16 oz.) cans apricot
halves, undrained
2 env. unflavored gelatin
5 egg yolks
1 1/4 c. sugar, divided
1/8 tsp. salt
1 c. milk

2 T. apricot brandy or light rum
1 (2 oz.) pkg. slivered almonds
1 1/2 c. whipping cream
3/4 c. whipping cream
2 T. powdered sugar
1/8 tsp. almond extract
Garnishes: apricots, sliced,
almonds

CUT a 3-inch strip of waxed paper; line sides of a 9-inch springform pan with strip. Split ladyfingers in half lengthwise; line sides and bottom of pan with ladyfingers.
DRAIN apricots, reserving 1/2 cup of juice. Set aside 4 apricots for garnish. Place knife blade in bowl of food processor; add remaining apricots and process 1 minute. Set aside.
SPRINKLE gelatin over reserved 1/2 cup apricot juice. Set aside.
COMBINE egg yolks, 3/4 cup sugar and salt in a heavy saucepan.
GRADUALLY add milk; cook over medium heat, stirring constantly, about 4 minutes, or until mixture thickens and thermometer reaches 160°.
ADD softened gelatin, stirring until gelatin dissolves.
STIR in puréed apricots, brandy and slivered almonds. Chill mixture until the consistency of unbeaten egg whites (about 30 minutes).
BEAT 1 1/2 cups whipping cream until foamy; gradually add remaining 1/2 cup sugar, beating until soft peaks form.
FOLD whipped cream into apricot mixture; spoon into springform pan. CHILL 8 hours.
REMOVE ring from springform pan; remove wax paper.
BEAT 3/4 cup whipping cream until foamy; gradually add powdered sugar and almond extract, beating until soft peaks form. Pipe or dollop on top of mousse. Slice remaining apricots; arrange on whipped cream. GARNISH, if desired.
YIELD: 10 servings.

Desserts

Baked Christmas Pudding Cake

1/2 c. granulated sugar
1/2 c. brown sugar
1 egg
2 T. melted butter
1 1/2 c. flour
1 tsp. baking soda
1/2 tsp. salt

1/2 tsp. baking powder
1 c. nuts
1 1/2 c. applesauce
1 c. raisins
1/4 c. red cherries
1/4 c. green cherries

MIX all ingredients.
POUR into greased and floured 7 x 11 x 1 1/2-inch baking pan.

TOPPING:
1 1/2 c. boiling water

1 1/2 c. brown sugar
1 T. butter

COMBINE ingredients; pour over cake.
BAKE at 375° for 40 minutes.
SERVE with whipped cream or ice cream.
YIELD: 8 to 10 servings.

Banana Cake

2/3 c. shortening	1 1/4 tsp. baking powder
1 2/3 c. sugar	1 tsp. salt
2 egg yolks + 1 whole egg	1 tsp. baking soda
1 1/4 c. mashed bananas	2/3 c. buttermilk
2 1/2 c. sifted flour	

STIR shortening until softened, then cream together with sugar.
ADD eggs and mix well.
STIR in bananas.
IN a separate bowl, sift together all dry ingredients.
SLOWLY add dry ingredients to shortening mixture, alternating with buttermilk.
BEAT vigorously for 2 minutes.
BAKE in two waxed-paper-lined layer cake pans at 350° for about 35 minutes.
COOL 10 minutes before removing from pans.

FROSTING:	1 T. vanilla
1 pt. whipping cream	3/4 c. powdered sugar
2 egg whites	Bananas, sliced

BEAT whipping cream and egg whites until stiff peaks form. While still beating, add vanilla and powdered sugar.
CONTINUE to beat until mixed well, but before butter begins to form.
SPRINKLE banana slices over top of first layer, then top with frosting.
COVER with second layer, sprinkle with bananas and top with frosting.
REFRIGERATE until ready to serve.

Bourbon-Chocolate Pecan Tarts

Cream Cheese Pastry*
  (see below)
3/4 c. (4.5 oz.) semi-sweet
  chocolate morsels
1/3 c. sugar
3 T. firmly-packed light
  brown sugar
1 T. all-purpose flour

3/4 c. light corn syrup
1/2 c. butter or margarine, melted
3 T. bourbon
2 tsp. vanilla extract
2 c. pecan halves
Garnishes: whipped cream, pecan
  halves, chopped pecans

DIVIDE pastry into 6 portions and shape each into a ball; press each into a 4 1/2-inch tart pan.
SPRINKLE chocolate morsels over pastry; chill 30 minutes.
BEAT eggs and next 7 ingredients at medium speed with an electric mixer until blended.
POUR into tart shells, filling each half-full.
ARRANGE pecan halves over filling; drizzle with remaining filling.
BAKE at 350° for 30 to 35 minutes, or until set; cool.
GARNISH, if desired.

CREAM CHEESE PASTRY:
1 (3 oz.) pkg. cream cheese,
  softened

1 c. all-purpose flour
1/2 c. butter or margarine,
  softened

BEAT cream cheese and butter at medium speed with a mixer until smooth.
ADD flour; beat at low speed until a soft dough forms.
YIELD: enough for 6 (4 1/2-inch) tarts.

Chocolate Fruitcake

1 c. butter or margarine
6 (1 oz.) sq. semi-sweet
  chocolate
1 1/4 c. sugar
3 lg. eggs
1 c. all-purpose flour
1/4 tsp. salt

1 c. red candied cherries, cut
  in half
1 c. green candied pineapple,
  cut into 1/2" wedges
3/4 c. walnut halves
3/4 c. pecan halves
Garnishes: red candied cherries,
  greenery, fresh holly

MELT butter and chocolate in a heavy saucepan over low heat, stirring often,
REMOVE from heat and cool about 15 minutes.
STIR in sugar.
ADD eggs, one at a time, stirring well after each addition.
ADD flour and salt, stirring until blended.
STIR in cherries and next 3 ingredients. Spoon mixture into 4 greased and floured 5 3/4 x 3 1/4 x 2-inch loaf pans.
BAKE at 350° for 35 minutes, or until a wooden toothpick inserted in center comes out clean. Cool in pans on wire racks 10 minutes; remove from pans and cool on wire racks.
SEAL cakes in heavy-duty plastic wrap and refrigerate 8 hours before cutting.
YIELD: 4 (12-ounce) loaves.

Chocolate Mousse in Phyllo

6 (18x12") sheets phyllo
6 T. butter or margarine,
   melted
5 egg whites
1 env. unflavored gelatin
1 (6 oz.) pkg. semi-sweet
   chocolate pieces
1/2 c. butter or margarine

1 tsp. instant coffee crystals
4 egg yolks
1/4 c. brandy
1/2 c. sugar
1 T. sugar
Whipped cream
Toasted almond slices

GENEROUSLY grease (or use nonstick vegetable spray) a 9-inch round cake pan with removable bottom (springform pan).

STACK phyllo sheets in bottom and up sides of pan, brushing each with some of melted butter or margarine and letting the sheets overlap pan edges.

TRIM dough to pan edge; crumble trimmings into pan.

BRUSH trimmings with remaining melted butter.

BAKE at 375° for 20 minutes, or until puffed and golden (crust will flatten on cooling).

COMBINE 1 egg white and 1 tablespoon of water; immediately brush over hot crust. Cool.

IN a small saucepan, soften gelatin in 1/3 cup cold water. Heat and stir until melted. Remove from heat; set aside.

IN top of double boiler, combine the egg yolks and brandy; beat until frothy with electric mixer.

GRADUALLY beat in the 1/2 cup of sugar until yolks are thick and lemon-colored.

PLACE over simmering water (upper pan should not touch water).

COOK and stir about 8 minutes, or just until slightly thickened. <u>Do not overcook</u>.

PLACE pan over cold water; beat 3 to 4 minutes, or until consistency of mayonnaise. Stir chocolate mixture into yolk mixture.

WASH beaters well, and beat remaining egg whites to soft peaks (tips curl over); gradually add remaining sugar, beating to stiff peaks.

FOLD chocolate mixture into egg white mixture. Pour into baked crust.

CHILL, covered, at least 3 hours, or overnight.

TO serve, remove from pan; top with whipped cream and sliced toasted almonds.

CUT into thin wedges.

YIELD: 12 servings.

Desserts

157

Chocolate-Praline Pie

1 recipe for single-crust
  pie (see recipe below)
Semi-sweet chocolate pieces
3 eggs
1 c. light corn syrup
1/2 c. sugar

2 T. praline liqueur or Amaretto
1 c. pecan halves
1/2 c. semi-sweet chocolate
  pieces
1/3 c. margarine or butter,
  melted

PREPARE the pastry. On lightly-floured surface, flatten the dough with hands. Roll the dough from the center to the edge, forming a circle about 12 inches in diameter. Ease the pastry into a 9-inch pie plate, being careful to avoid stretching the pastry. Trim the crust evenly with the edge of the pie plate.

REROLL the dough scraps. Use an hors d'oeuvre cutter to make cutouts from the scraps. Brush the edge of pastry with water. Arrange cutouts and chocolate pieces around the edge. Do not prick pastry.

FOR FILLING:
IN a mixing bowl, beat the eggs slightly with a rotary beater or a fork.
STIR in the corn syrup.
ADD the sugar, margarine or butter, and praline liqueur or Amaretto, stirring until sugar is dissolved.
STIR in the pecans and 1/2 cup of chocolate pieces.
PLACE the pastry-lined pie plate on oven rack.
POUR the filling into the plate.
TO prevent the pastry from overbrowning, cover the edge of the pie with a piece of foil.
BAKE in a 350° oven for 35 minutes.
REMOVE the foil.
BAKE for 20 to 25 minutes more, or until knife inserted near the center of the pie comes out clean.
COOL pie thoroughly on a wire rack before serving.
COVER the pie; chill in the refrigerator to store.
YIELD: 8 servings.

Continued on following page.

Desserts

Continued from preceding page.

PASTRY FOR SINGLE-CRUST PIE:
IN a medium mixing bowl, stir together 1 1/4 cups all-purpose flour and 1/2 teaspoon salt.
CUT in 1/3 cup shortening until the pieces are the size of small peas.
SPRINKLE 1 tablespoon cold water over part of the flour and shortening mixture.
GENTLY toss with a fork; push mixture to the side of the bowl.
REPEAT until all is moistened (3 to 4 tablespoons of water total).
FORM dough into a ball.

Desserts

Christmas Cake

3 c. sifted cake flour, or	2 tsp. vanilla
2 1/2 c. all-purpose flour	1 1/3 c. half & half
4 tsp. baking powder	8 egg whites
1 c. butter	1 c. sugar
1 c. sugar	

GREASE and lightly flour three 9 x 1 1/2-inch or 8 x 1 1/2-inch round cake pans; set aside.

SIFT together the cake flour, baking powder and salt into a medium bowl; set aside.

IN a large mixing bowl, beat butter with an electric mixer for 30 seconds.

ADD 1 cup sugar and the vanilla; beat until fluffy.

ADD the dry ingredients alternately with cream to creamed mixture, beating on low to medium speed after each addition, until just combined.

CLEAN beaters. In another large mixing bowl, beat egg whites on medium to high speed until soft peaks form (tips curl).

GRADUALLY add 1 cup sugar and beat on high speed until stiff peaks form (tips stand straight), but the egg whites aren't dry.

GENTLY fold the egg whites, a little at a time, into cake batter.

DIVIDE the cake batter into the 3 prepared pans.

BAKE at 350° for about 30 minutes for 8-inch and 25 minutes for 9-inch, or until a toothpick comes out clean.

COOL layers in pans on wire racks for 10 minutes.

REMOVE layers from pans and completely cool on wire rack.

YOU may use any icing you choose.

WHITE ICING:

18 oz. white chocolate baking	1 (3oz.) pkg. cream cheese
squares, chopped	1 1/2 c. butter, cut into pieces

IN a heavy saucepan, melt chocolate over low heat.

COOL until slightly warm.

IN a large mixing bowl, beat cream cheese with an electric mixer until smooth.

ADD butter; beat until fluffy.

GRADUALLY add cooled chocolate, beating until well blended.

MAKES enough frosting for a 9-inch 3-layer cake or a large sheet cake, 17 1/4 x 11 1/2 inches.

Christmas Pears with Creme Chantilly

1/4 c. water
1/4 c. sugar
2 T. lemon juice
1/4 tsp. ground mace
6 to 8 med. pears

1 (1 oz.) pkg. frozen raspberries,
  thawed
Creme Chantilly (see recipe
  below)

COMBINE water, sugar, lemon juice and ground mace in a shallow 2-quart casserole, stirring until sugar dissolves; set aside.
PEEL pears, leaving stems intact. Place pears in sugar mixture; spoon over pears.
COVER and bake at 350° for 50 minutes, or until pears are tender, but hold their shape. Carefully remove pears from sugar mixture. Discard sugar mixture; return pears to casserole.
PLACE raspberries in a strainer over a bowl; mash berries with the back of a spoon. Discard seeds. Pour raspberry juice over pears; cover and refrigerate 8 hours, spooning juice over pears occasionally.
TO serve, spoon about 3 tablespoons Creme Chantilly on individual plates, and place pear upright on creme.
YIELD: 6 to 8 servings.

CREME CHANTILLY:
1 c. whipping cream

1/2 tsp. vanilla extract
1 to 2 T. powdered sugar

BEAT all ingredients at medium speed with an electric mixer until thickened, but not stiff.
YIELD: 1 1/2 cups.

NOTE: This recipe calls for mace. This is a spice a lot of people are not familiar with, therefore, avoid recipes that call for it. Mace has a flavor of nutmeg, is very light and good.

Coconut Crunch Torte

1 c. flaked coconut	1 tsp. vanilla
1/2 c. graham cracker crumbs	1/2 tsp. salt
1/3 c. chopped cashew nuts	1 c. sugar
4 egg whites	Thawed vanilla ice cream

IN a small bowl, combine coconut, graham cracker crumbs and cashews. Set aside.

IN a large mixer bowl, beat egg whites, vanilla and salt until soft peaks form (tips curl over).

ADD sugar, a tablespoon at a time, beating until stiff peaks form (tips stand upright).

FOLD in coconut mixture.

SPREAD in a well-greased 9-inch pie plate.

BAKE in a 350° oven for 30 to 35 minutes, or until lightly browned.

PLACE on wire rack and cool completely.

TO SERVE, cut torte in wedges and top with soft vanilla ice cream, with cashew pieces on top.

YIELD: 6 to 8 servings.

NOTE: This is a great addition to any holiday party, easy to make and extra easy to serve.

Coffee Coconut Mousse

2/3 c. sugar
2 T. instant coffee granules
1 env. unflavored gelatin

1 (3 oz.) can flaked coconut,
 toasted
2 c. whipping cream
3/4 c. milk

IN a 2-quart saucepan, combine sugar, coffee granules, gelatin and dash of salt.

ADD milk.

HEAT, stirring constantly, until the sugar and coffee granules and gelatin are dissolved.

CHILL until mixture is partially thickened (consistency of unbeaten egg whites).

WHIP cream just to soft peaks.

FOLD cream into the gelatin mixture along with 1 cup of the coconut.

PLACE 2-inch-wide strips of foil around 1/2-cup soufflé dishes so that it extends 1 inch above the rim; tape to secure.

SPOON in coconut mixture, piling to top of collar (or turn mixture into foil-lined loaf pan). Cover and freeze firm.

LET mousse stand for 10 minutes at room temperature before serving.

REMOVE foil collars from soufflé dishes, or spoon into sherbet glasses.

SPRINKLE remaining coconut atop, and garnish with a maraschino cherry.

YIELD: 8 servings.

Cranberry Dessert Loaf

2 (3 oz.) pkg. cream cheese, softened	1 1/2 tsp. baking powder
	1/2 tsp. baking soda
1 egg	1/2 tsp. salt
2 T. orange liqueur or apple juice	3/4 c. apple juice
	1/4 c. butter, melted
1 T. sugar	1 beaten egg
2 c. all-purpose flour	1 1/2 c. chopped fresh
1 c. sugar	cranberries

GREASE and lightly flour a 9x5x3-inch loaf pan. Set aside.

IN a small bowl, beat cream cheese with electric mixer until light and fluffy.

ADD 1 egg, orange liqueur (or apple juice) and 1 tablespoon sugar.

BEAT until well combined.

IN a large bowl, stir together the flour, 1 cup sugar, baking powder, baking soda and salt.

STIR in apple juice, butter and beaten eggs.

FOLD in the cranberries and walnuts.

SPOON half of the batter into the prepared pan.

SPOON cream cheese mixture evenly over the batter. Top with remaining batter.

BaKE in a 350° oven for 65 to 75 minutes.

COOL for 15 minutes in the pan on a wire rack.

REMOVE from pan and cool on rack.

WHEN completely cool, wrap tightly in clear plastic wrap.

STORE in the refrigerator for up to 1 week.

OR store in the freezer for up to 3 months.

YIELD: 16 servings.

Cranberry Mousse

1/2 c. sugar	2 egg whites
1 env. unflavored gelatin	2 T. sugar
1/4 tsp. finely-shredded	1/2 c. whipping cream
orange peel	Raspberry Sauce (see recipe
1/2 c. orange juice	below)
2 c. fresh cranberries	Fresh mint leaves (opt.)

IN a medium saucepan, combine the 1/2 cup sugar and gelatin. Stir in orange juice.

COOK and stir over medium heat until gelatin is dissolved.

STIR in orange peel and cranberries. Bring to boiling; reduce heat. Cover; simmer about 5 minutes, or until cranberry skins pop.

TRANSFER the cranberry-gelatin mixture to a medium mixing bowl. Chill until the mixture is cool and thickened, stirring occasionally. Remove from the refrigerator (mixture will continue to set.)

IN a small mixer bowl, immediately beat egg whites with an electric mixer on medium speed, until soft peaks form (tips curl).

GRADUALLY add the 2 tablespoons sugar, beating on high speed until stiff peaks form (tips stand straight).

WHEN gelatin mixture is partially set (the consistency of unbeaten egg whites), fold in stiff-beaten egg whites.

IN a small mixer bowl, beat the whipping cream with an electric mixer on low speed until soft peaks form. Fold in gelatin mixture.

CHILL until mixture mounds when spooned. Spoon into a 1-quart glass bowl. Chill for several hours or until firm.

TO SERVE, spoon onto dessert plates; top with Raspberry Sauce. Garnish with mint leaves, if desired.

YIELD: 6 servings.

RASPBERRY SAUCE:

SIEVE 1 (10-ounce) package frozen raspberries, thawed; discard seeds. ADD water to make 1 cup.

IN a small saucepan, combine raspberry juice, 2 tablespoons sugar and 2 teaspoons cornstarch.

Cook and stir over medium-high heat until bubbly; cook and stir for 2 minutes more.

STIR in 2 teaspoons vanilla.

COVER; chill.

Desserts   **165**

Cranberry Torte

1 1/2 c. graham cracker crumbs	1/4 c. sugar
1/2 c. chopped pecans	6 T. butter or margarine, melted

IN mixing bowl, combine graham cracker crumbs, pecans, the 1/4 cup sugar and the melted butter or margarine.

PRESS onto bottom and up sides of an 8-inch springform pan.

CHILL.

1 1/2 c. ground fresh cranberries (2 c. whole berries)	1 tsp. vanilla
	1/8 tsp. salt
1 c. sugar	1 c. whipping cream
2 egg whites	1 recipe Cranberry Glaze (see recipe below)
1 T. frozen orange juice concentrate, thawed	Fresh orange slices, quartered

IN a mixing bowl, combine cranberries and the 1 cup sugar; let stand 5 minutes.

ADD unbeaten egg whites, orange juice concentrate, vanilla and salt.

BEAT on low speed of electric mixer until frothy.

THEN beat at high speed 6 to 8 minutes, or until stiff peaks form (tips stand straight).

IN a small mixer bowl, whip cream to soft peaks (tips curl over); fold into cranberry mixture.

TURN into crust. Freeze firm.

TO SERVE, remove torte from pan. Place on serving plate.

SPOON Cranberry Glaze in center; place orange slices around outside.

YIELD: 8 to 10 servings.

CRANBERRY GLAZE:

1/2 c. sugar	3/4 c. fresh cranberries
1 T. cornstarch	2/3 c. water

IN a saucepan, stir together sugar and cornstarch; stir in cranberries and water.

COOK and stir until bubbly.

COOK, stirring occasionally, just until cranberry skins pop.

COOL to room temperature (do not chill).

YIELD: 1 cup.

Desserts

Cream Cheese Pound Cake

1 1/2 c. butter, softened	6 lg. eggs
1 (8 oz.) pkg. cream cheese,	1 1/2 tsp. vanilla extract
softened	3 c. all-purpose flour
3 c. sugar	1/8 tsp. salt

BEAT butter and cream cheese at medium speed with an electric mixer 2 minutes, or until creamy. Gradually add sugar, beating 5 to 7 minutes.
ADD eggs, one at a time, beating just until yellow disappears.
ADD vanilla, mixing well.
COMBINE flour and salt; gradually add to butter mixture, beating at low speed just until blended, after each addition.
POUR batter into a greased and floured 10-inch tube pan.
FILL a 2-cup, ovenproof measuring cup with water; place in oven with tube pan.
BAKE at 300° for 1 hour and 30 minutes, or until a wooden pick inserted in center of cake comes out clean.
COOL in pan on a wire rack 10 to 15 minutes; remove from pan and cool completely on wire rack.
YIELD: 1 (10-inch) cake.

NOTE: This pound cake can be used in any number of ways; you can start with it as a base and use your imagination to create your own tastes.

Fruitcake

6 egg yolks	3/4 tsp. salt
3/4 c. cherry juice or wine	2 lb. dates
3 T. butter, melted	1 lb. Brazil nuts
2 1/4 c. sugar	1 lb. English walnuts
2 tsp. vanilla	3 bottles maraschino cherries,
3 c. flour	drained
1 1/2 tsp. baking powder	6 egg whites, beaten

BEAT egg yolks; add juice, butter, sugar and vanilla.
MIX flour, baking powder and salt.
WITH fruit and nuts, add 1 cup of flour. Mix all.
FOLD in egg whites; will be very stiff and thick.
BAKE at 300° up to 2 hours, until done.
COOL and wrap in a cheesecloth soaked in wine.

Desserts   167

Fruitcake

4 c. all-purpose flour,
divided
1 lb. chopped dates
1 lb. candied citron
1 lb. chopped pecans
1 lb. dried figs, coarsely
chopped
1 (15 oz.) pkg. raisins
1 (10 oz.) pkg. currants
1 c. butter or margarine, softened
2 c. sugar
12 lg. eggs, lightly beaten

1 c. milk
3/4 c. light corn syrup
2 tsp. baking soda
2 tsp. ground nutmeg
2 tsp. ground cinnamon
2 tsp. ground allspice
1 tsp. baking powder
1 c. brandy
15 pecan halves
Brandy
3 red candied cherry halves
(opt.)

MAKE a liner for a 10-inch tube pan by drawing an 18-inch circle on brown paper (not recycled). Cut out circle; set pan in center and draw around base of pan and inside tube. Remove pan and fold circle into eighths, with lines on the outside.

CUT off pointed tip of triangle along line. Unfold paper; cut along folds to the outside line. Place liner in pan; grease and set aside. Repeat process for second pan.

COMBINE 1/2 cup flour, dates and next 5 ingredients in a large bowl, tossing gently to coat. Set aside.

BEAT butter at medium speed with electric mixer until creamy; gradually add sugar, beating well. Add eggs, beating until blended after each addition.

ADD milk and corn syrup, mixing well.

COMBINE remaining 3 1/2 cups flour, baking soda and next 4 ingredients.

ADD to butter mixture alternately with 1 cup brandy, beginning and ending with flour mixture.

MIX at low speed after each addition until blended.

POUR over fruit mixture; stir well.

SPOON batter into prepared pans. Place pecan halves in flower designs on top of batter, if desired.

BAKE at 350° for 1 hour, or until a wooden pick inserted in center of cake comes out clean. Remove from oven; cool completely in pans on wire racks.

REMOVE cake from pans; peel paper from cakes.

WRAP in brandy-soaked cheesecloth; store in airtight containers in a cool place. Pour a little brandy over cakes each week for at least 1 month. Before serving, place cherry halves in center of pecan flowers, if desired.

YIELD: 2 (5-pound) cakes.

Desserts

Holiday Ice Cream Bombe

3 c. pistachio ice cream or
mint chocolate chip ice
cream
3 c. vanilla ice cream
1/3 c. diced mixed candied
fruits & peels

1 qt. chocolate or chocolate
fudge ice cream
Pistachio nuts (opt.)
Chocolate Leaves (opt.)
(see recipe below)
1 recipe Chocolate Sauce
(see recipe below)

IN a chilled mixing bowl, stir pistachio ice cream just to soften. Spread evenly in the bottom of a 2-quart mold. Freeze for 30 minutes.

MEANWHILE, in a chilled mixing bowl, stir vanilla ice cream just to soften. STIR in candied fruits and peels.

SPREAD evenly over pistachio ice cream layer. Freeze for 30 minutes. IN a chilled mixing bowl, stir chocolate ice cream just to soften. Spread evenly over vanilla ice cream layer. Cover and freeze several hours, or up to 1 month.

TO SERVE, wrap a hot, damp towel around mold for several seconds. Center an upside-down serving platter over the mold. Holding tightly, invert the plate and mold. Lift off the mold. Garnish with pistachio nuts and Chocolate Leaves, if desired. Serve at once with Chocolate Sauce. YIELD: 10 servings.

CHOCOLATE LEAVES:

IN a heavy saucepan, cook 2 squares (2 ounces) semi-sweet chocolate over low heat, stirring constantly until the chocolate begins to melt. Immediately remove the chocolate from the heat and stir until smooth. WITH a small paintbrush, brush melted chocolate on the underside of nontoxic fresh leaves (such as lemon, mint or ivy), building up layers of chocolate so garnish will be sturdy.

WIPE off chocolate that may have run onto the front of the leaves. Place on a baking sheet lined with waxed paper; chill or freeze until hardened. Just before using, carefully peel the fresh leaves away from the chocolate leaves.

CHOCOLATE SAUCE:

IN a small saucepan, combine 8 squares (8 ounces) cut-up semi-sweet chocolate and 2/3 cup light cream.

COOK over medium-low heat until slightly thickened and bubbly. REMOVE from heat, stir in 1 teaspoon vanilla. SERVE warm. YIELD: 1 cup.

Desserts

Italian Cheesecake with Ricotta Cheese

3/4 c. all-purpose flour
2 T. sugar
1/8 tsp. salt
1/3 c. butter or margarine, softened
2 1/2 c. ricotta cheese
1/2 c. sugar
3 T. all-purpose flour
3 lg. eggs
1 tsp. grated orange rind
1 tsp. vanilla extract
1/4 tsp. salt
2 T. golden raisins
2 T. finely-chopped candied citron
2 T. chopped almonds
Garnishes: orange sections, orange rind strips

COMBINE the first 3 ingredients in a small bowl; cut in butter with a pastry blender until mixture is crumbly. Press mixture into a 9-inch springform pan.

BAKE at 475° for 5 minutes. Cool on a wire rack.

COMBINE ricotta cheese, 1/2 cup sugar and 3 tablespoons flour; beat at medium speed with an electric mixer until smooth.

ADD eggs and next 3 ingredients; beat 4 minutes. Stir in raisins, citron and almonds and spoon over crust.

BAKE at 350° for 1 hour to 1 hour and 15 minutes, or until center is set.

RUN a knife around edge of cheesecake to loosen; cool in pan on a wire rack.

COVER and chill at least 8 hours. Carefully remove sides of pan just before serving.

GARNISH, if desired.

YIELD: 12 to 16 servings.

Mincemeat Brown Betty

2 c. coarse dry bread crumbs	1/4 tsp. salt
4 apples, sliced in eighths	3 T. lemon juice
1 c. prepared mincemeat	1/4 c. water
1/2 c. sugar	2 T. butter or margarine
1/4 tsp. ground cinnamon	

PLACE 1/3 of crumbs into bottom of buttered 1 1/2 to 2-quart casserole; cover with half of apples and half of mincemeat.

MIX together sugar, cinnamon and salt; sprinkle half over mincemeat.

ADD layer of crumbs; then one of apples and mincemeat; sprinkle with remaining sugar mixture.

TOP with remaining crumbs; pour lemon juice and water over all; dot with butter.

COVER: bake at 350° for 20 minutes; uncover; bake 15 minutes longer.

SERVE hot or cold, plain or with whipped cream.

YIELD: 4 to 5 servings.

Mincemeat Pie

1 (23 oz.) can mincemeat pie filling	2 c. sliced cooking apples
1 (8 oz.) can crushed pineapple, drained	1 (15 oz.) pkg. refrigerated pie crusts, or your own recipe
	1 T. sugar

COMBINE the first 3 ingredients in a large bowl; set aside.

FIT 1 pie crust into a 9-inch pie plate. Spoon mincemeat mixture into prepared pie crust.

ROLL remaining pie crust; cut with a leaf-shaped cutter. Mark veins on leaves with a pastry wheel or sharp knife. Arrange pastry leaves on mincemeat mixture; sprinkle pie with sugar.

BAKE at 425° for 30 to 32 minutes, or until golden, shielding edges with strips of foil after 12 minutes, to prevent excessive browning.

YIELD: 1 (9-inch) pie.

Pear and Mincemeat Pie

Pastry for double-crust,   1 (17 oz.) jar mincemeat, with
    9" pie   brandy and rum
2 lb. firm ripe pears   2 T. heavy cream

ON a lightly floured surface, roll out 2/3 of dough to 1/8-inch thickness.

FIT into a 9-inch pie plate.

TRIM pastry edges.

WRAP remaining dough in plastic wrap. Set aside.

CUT 2 pounds firm, ripe pears into quarters, pare and remove cores.

CUT each quarter into 3 slices and arrange over bottom of pastry-lined plate.

TOP pears with the jar of mincemeat with brandy and rum.

MOISTEN rim of crust with water.

ROLL out remaining dough and place on top of pie.

Trim crust to hang over no more than 1/4-inch.

TURN edge under and flute.

CUT 2 or 3 slits in top crust to allow steam to escape.

BRUSH pastry with 2 tablespoons heavy cream.

BAKE at 425° for 30 to 35 minutes, until crust is deep golden brown.

SERVE hot or cold.

YIELD: 6 to 8 servings.

Pumpkin Cheesecake

3/4 c. crushed gingersnaps
1/2 c. toasted, ground
  almonds
1/4 c. butter, melted
3 (8 oz.) pkg. cream cheese
1/2 c. granulated sugar
1/2 c. packed brown sugar
2 T. cognac, brandy or milk

4 eggs
1 1/2 c. canned pumpkin
1/4 c. sour cream
2 tsp. ground cinnamon
1/2 tsp. ground ginger
1/2 tsp. cardamom
1/4 tsp. cloves

CRUST: In a bowl, combine gingersnaps and almonds.
STIR in butter.
PRESS onto bottom and 1 inch up sides of a 9- or 10-inch springform pan.
FILLING: In a large mixing bowl, beat cream cheese, sugar and cognac with an electric mixer until combined.
STIR in the pumpkin, sour cream, cinnamon, ginger, cardamom and cloves.
POUR filling into crust-lined pan.
PLACE in a shallow baking pan.
BAKE in a 375° oven for 55 to 60 minutes for 9-inch pan, or 35 to 40 minutes for 10-inch pan, or until the center appears nearly set when you gently shake it.
COOL in pan on a wire rack for 15 minutes. Loosen crust from sides of pan. Cool 30 minutes more.
REMOVE sides of pan; cool cheesecake completely.
COVER; chill at least 4 hours before serving.
SERVE with whipped half & half or ice cream.
SPRINKLE top with crushed gingersnaps or sugared pecans.
YIELD: 12 to 16 servings.

Pumpkin Roll

3 eggs
1 c. sugar
2/3 c. mashed, cooked
  pumpkin
1 tsp. lemon juice
3/4 c. all-purpose flour
1 tsp. baking powder
1/4 tsp. salt
1 tsp. ground cinnamon
1 tsp. pumpkin pie spice
1/4 tsp. ground nutmeg

1 c. chopped pecans
1 to 2 T. powdered sugar
1 (8 oz.) pkg. cream cheese,
  softened
1/3 c. butter or margarine,
  softened
1 c. sifted powdered sugar
1 tsp. vanilla extract
Garnishes: sweetened whipped
  cream, chopped pecans

GREASE and flour a 10x15x1-inch jellyroll pan; set aside.

BEAT eggs in a large bowl at high speed with an electric mixer until thick; gradually add sugar and beat 5 additional minutes.

STIR in pumpkin and lemon juice.

COMBINE flour and next 5 ingredients; gradually stir into pumpkin mixture.

SPREAD batter evenly in prepared pan; sprinkle with 1 cup pecans, gently pressing into batter.

BAKE at 375° for 12 to 15 minutes.

SIFT 1 to 2 tablespoons powdered sugar in a 10x15-inch rectangle on a cloth towel.

WHEN cake is done, immediately loosen from sides of pan and turn cake out onto sugared towel. Starting at the narrow end, roll up cake and towel together; let cake cool on a wire rack, seam-side down.

BEAT cream cheese and butter in a large bowl, at high speed with an electric mixer; gradually add 1 cup powdered sugar and vanilla, beating until blended.

UNROLL cake; spread with cream cheese mixture and carefully reroll.

PLACE cake on plate, seam-side down. Garnish with whipped cream and/or pecans, if desired.

YIELD: 10 servings.

Red Velvet Christmas Cake

This cake has always been my sons' birthday cake, the oldest was born just before Christmas, and the youngest in January. My husband's mother made this cake for our oldest the first time, and it has been our official "Red Birthday Cake" ever since.

1/2 c. shortening	1 c. buttermilk
1 1/2 c. sugar	1 tsp. vanilla
2 eggs	2 1/2 c. cake flour
2 oz. red food coloring	1 tsp. baking soda
2 T. cocoa	1 tsp. vinegar
1 tsp. salt	

CREAM shortening and sugar; add eggs, one at a time.
STIR in food coloring and vanilla, blending well.
COMBINE flour, salt and cocoa; set aside.
COMBINE buttermilk, vinegar and baking soda in a 4-cup liquid measuring cup (mixture will bubble).
ADD flour mixture to shortening mixture, alternately with buttermilk mixture.
BEAT at low speed until blended after each addition.
BEAT at medium speed 2 minutes; pour batter into 3 greased and floured 8-inch round cake pans.
BAKE at 350° for 25 minutes.
COOL in pans on wire racks 10 minutes; remove from pans and cool completely on wire racks.
SPREAD frosting (see recipe below) between layers and on top of cake.
GARNISH as desired.

FROSTING:	1 c. margarine
3 T. flour	1 c. sugar
1 c. milk	1 tsp. vanilla

COOK flour and milk until thick (stir while cooking, or it will get lumpy; stir also while cooling).
COOL.
CREAM margarine, sugar and vanilla; beat with electric mixer for about 5 minutes, or until fluffy and sugar is no longer grainy.
ADD cooled milk mixture and beat well, until smooth and fluffy.

Desserts

Rum-Walnut Pumpkin Pie

Pastry for 1-crust 9" pie
1 1/2 cans pumpkin
3/4 c. packed brown sugar
1 tsp. ground cinnamon
1/2 sp. ground ginger
1/2 tsp. ground nutmeg

3 eggs
1 c. evaporated milk
3 T. dark rum
3/4 c. chopped walnuts
1/2 c. whipping cream
2 tsp. granulated sugar

PREPARE and roll out pastry. Line a 9-inch pie plate with pastry; trim pastry to 1/2-inch beyond edge. Flute edge high; do not prick.

IN bowl, combine pumpkin, brown sugar, cinnamon, 1/2 teaspoon salt, ginger and nutmeg.

LIGHTLY beat eggs into mixture with fork.

STIR in evaporated milk and rum; mix well.

STIR in nuts.

PLACE pie plate on oven rack; pour pumpkin mixture into shell.

TO prevent overbrowning, cover edge of pie with foil.

BAKE in 375° oven for 25 minutes.

REMOVE foil; bake 20 to 25 minutes more, or until a knife inserted just off-center comes out clean.

COOL on rack.

BEAT cream with granulated sugar, on high speed of an electric mixer, to soft peaks.

SPOON on top of cool pie.

Spiceless Fruitcake

6 eggs
1 1/2 c. flour
1 1/2 c. sugar
1 1/2 tsp. baking powder
1 1/2 lb. dates, chopped
1 1/2 c. English walnuts, chopped

1 1/2 c. maraschino cherries, halved
1 1/2 c. Brazil nuts, chopped
6 T. cherry juice
2 c. pecans, chopped

BEAT egg yolks until light (reserving whites); add sugar, juice, flour and baking powder.
ADD remaining ingredients.
BEAT reserved egg whites to stiff peaks and fold into mixture.
LINE the bottom of 4 (1-pound) loaf pans with waxed paper; fill evenly with batter.
BAKE at 250° for 1 1/2 to 2 hours.

Sweet Potato Pie

2 c. cooked, mashed sweet potatoes
1 c. firmly-packed brown sugar
1/2 c. butter or margarine, softened
2 eggs, separated
1/2 tsp. ground ginger

1/2 tsp. ground cinnamon
1/2 tsp. ground nutmeg
1/4 tsp. salt
1/2 c. evaporated milk
1/4 c. sugar
1 unbaked 10" pastry shell
Whipped topping (opt.)

COMBINE sweet potatoes, brown sugar, butter, egg yolks, spices and salt in a large mixing bowl; beat until light and fluffy.
ADD evaporated milk; beat just until blended.
BEAT egg whites (at room temperature) until foamy; gradually add sugar, 1 tablespoon at a time, beating until stiff peaks form. Fold into potato mixture.
POUR filling into pastry shell.
BAKE at 400° for 10 minutes; reduce heat to 350° and bake an additional 45 to 50 minutes, or until set. Cool.
TOP with dollops of whipped topping, if desired.

Desserts

177

Walnut Pie

1/2 c. brown sugar	3 eggs
2 T. all-purpose flour	1 1/2 tsp. vanilla
1 1/4 c. light corn syrup	1 unbaked 9" pie shell
3 T. butter	1 c. large pieces walnuts
1/4 tsp. salt	

MIX brown sugar and flour in saucepan.
ADD corn syrup, butter and salt; warm over low heat just until butter is melted.
BEAT eggs with vanilla.
STIR in sugar mixture.
BAKE on lower rack of oven at 375° for 40 to 45 minutes, until filling is set in center.
COOL.
YIELD: 1 (9-inch) pie.

Desserts

White Fruitcake

2 lb. white raisins, chopped
2 c. orange juice
4 1/2 c. sifted cake flour
1/4 tsp. baking powder
1/2 tsp. salt
1 lb. diced candied cherries
1 lb. diced candied pineapple
1/2 lb. diced preserved citron
1/4 lb. diced candied lemon
    peel
1/4 lb. diced candied orange
    peel
1 lb. almonds, blanched &
    slivered
2 c. butter or margarine
2 1/4 c. sugar
8 to 10 med.-size eggs
1 1/2 to 2 c. shredded coconut

WASH raisins; chop.
COMBINE with 1 cup orange juice; let stand overnight.
SAVE 1 1/2 cups flour to mix with candied fruit and nuts.
SIFT remaining 3 cups of flour with baking powder and salt.
MIX candied fruit and nuts with reserved 1 1/2 cups flour.
CREAM butter; add sugar and beat well.
ADD eggs, one at a time, beating well after each addition.
GRADUALLY add dry ingredients, beating after each addition.
ADD coconut, floured fruit and nuts, raisins and remaining orange juice.
BEAT well.
DIVIDE batter evenly in 2 well-greased 9- or 10-inch tube pans.
BAKE at 250° for about 2 1/2 hours, or until done.
OR, bake in 4 greased, paper-lined 9x5x3-inch loaf pans at the same temperature for the same length of time.
COOL 30 minutes on racks.
REMOVE from pans; cool completely.
WRAP in waxed paper or foil; store in airtight container in freezer.

Notes &
Recipes

_____

CANDIES AND COOKIES

List Your Favorite Recipes

Recipes   **Page**

_____   _____

_____   _____

_____   _____

_____   _____

_____   _____

_____   _____

_____   _____

_____   _____

_____   _____

_____   _____

_____   _____

_____   _____

_____   _____

_____   _____

_____   _____

_____   _____

_____   _____

_____   _____

Almond-Coconut Bark

2 c. sugar
1 c. evaporated milk
1/2 c. butter or margarine
8 oz. white almond bark

1 c. mini marshmallows
1/2 c. flaked coconut
1/2 c. chopped almonds
1 tsp. vanilla

BUTTER sides of heavy 3-quart saucepan; add sugar, evaporated milk and margarine. Cook over medium heat to soft ball stage, stirring frequently.
REMOVE from heat; add almond bark and marshmallows. Beat until melted.
QUICKLY stir in coconut, almonds and vanilla.
POUR into a 10x6x6-inch buttered glass baking dish.

Aunt Dodie's Stained Glass Windows

Another Recipe from Lois Jakoby.

1 (12 oz.) pkg. chocolate chips
1 stick margarine
1 c. chopped nuts

1 pkg. colored mini
marshmallows

MELT chocolate chips and margarine; cool until lukewarm.
ADD chopped nuts and marshmallows; blend well.
FORM mixture into 3 logs; roll in crushed nuts or coconut.
WRAP logs in foil or waxed paper and cool in refrigerator.
SLICE and serve.

Aunt Mary's Pecan-Filled Cookies

DOUGH:

1 stick margarine	1 c. flour
1 (3 oz.) pkg. cream cheese	A sm. pinch of salt

MIX all ingredients thoroughly; shape into little balls and press into miniature muffin tin. Press up sides to make a shell. (Muffin tins need to be 1-inch in diameter.)

FILLING:	1 T. margarine
3/4 c. brown sugar	1 tsp. vanilla
1 egg	1 c. pecans

MIX all ingredients well and place 1 teaspoon in each prepared shell.
BAKE at 375° for 25 minutes.
REMOVE from oven and sprinkle lightly with sifted powdered sugar, if desired.
YIELD: 24 cookies. (I always double this recipe.)

Biscochitos

This recipe is from Beverly Pareo, from Vequita, New Mexico. These are typical Mexican cookies made for Christmas. They are similar to a sugar cookie, but Beverly says, with a different flavor.

6 c. flour	2 eggs
2 c. lard (lard must be used)	3 tsp. baking powder
1 1/2 c. sugar	1/2 tsp. salt
2 tsp. anise seed	1 shot brandy or wine

CREAM lard and sugar.
ADD eggs.
ADD dry ingredients and flavoring.
MIX well; chill overnight.
ROLL out on floured surface, 1/4-inch thick.
CUT into circles; sprinkle or roll tops with 1 teaspoon cinnamon to 1/2 cup sugar.
BAKE at 375° for about 12 minutes.

Candies and Cookies

These cookie recipes are from my mother-in-law, Ione Schneckloth, she has many, many cookie recipes, these are two favorites.

Brown Sugar Cookies

2 c. brown sugar	3 1/2 c. flour
1 c. butter	1 c. nuts
2 eggs	1 tsp. cream of tartar
1 tsp. baking soda	1 tsp. salt
1 tsp. vanilla	

MIX the baking soda, flour, cream of tartar and salt together; set aside.
CREAM butter, eggs, brown sugar and vanilla.
COMBINE the creamed mixture with the flour mixture; mix well.
STIR in nuts; form dough into rolls.
WRAP rolls with waxed paper and refrigerate overnight.
NEXT day, slice to desired thickness, and bake at 350° for 8 to 10 minutes, or until edges are brown.

German Brown Cookies

1 c. butter	Pinch of salt
1 c. sugar	1/4 tsp. ginger
1 1/4 tsp. baking soda, mix	1/8 c. lemon rind
soda in a little hot water	1/4 tsp. cloves
& add to 1/2 c. molasses	1 tsp. cinnamon
1/8 c. orange rind	3 1/2 c. flour

MIX flour, orange rind, lemon rind, salt and spices; set aside.
CREAM together butter and sugar; add baking soda and molasses mixture; mix well.
COMBINE flour and creamed mixutre; mix well.
FORM into 2 long rolls, wrap in waxed paper and chill in refrigerator for several hours.
REMOVE from refrigerator, unwrap, slice, and bake at 350° for 8 to 10 minutes, or until lightly browned.

Butterscotch Candy

2 c. sugar	2 T. water
1/4 c. light corn syrup	2 T. vinegar
1/2 c. butter	

COMBINE all ingredients in a heavy 2-quart saucepan.
STIR and cook over medium heat until sugar is dissolved.
REDUCE heat and cook at medium boil, stirring as needed to control foaming.
IF sugar crystals form on side of pan, wipe off.
COOK to hard-crack stage (300°).
REMOVE from heat and let stand 1 minute.
BUTTER 2 sheets of aluminum foil on a cookie sheet, or butter the inside of muffin tins.
DROP by teaspoons onto foil, about 1/2-inch apart.
IF candy thickens so it won't drop, set in hot water to thin.
IF candy sticks to muffin tins, set in hot water and work loose with a knife.
YIELD: 6 dozen patties, or 1 1/2 pounds of candy.

Candy Cane Cookies

1 c. soft shortening	1 tsp. vanilla
1 c. sifted confectioners' sugar	2 1/2 c. sifted flour
1 egg	1 tsp. salt
1 1/2 tsp. almond flavor	1/2 tsp. red food coloring

HEAT oven to 375°.
MIX shortening, sugar, egg and flavoring well.
MIX flour and salt; stir into first mixture.
DIVIDE dough in half.
ADD coloring to half of dough, roll each lightly, and in strips 4 inches long.
PLACE strips side-by-side.
TWIST strips together and place on sheet, turning top over like candy cane.
BAKE 9 minutes.
YIELD: 4 dozen.

Candies and Cookies

Chocolate Bourbon Balls

1 c. semi-sweet chocolate
   chips
3 T. corn syrup
1/2 c. bourbon
2 1/2 c. vanilla wafer crumbs

1/2 c. sifted confectioners' sugar
1 c. nuts of choice, finely
   chopped
Granulated sugar, as needed

MELT chocolate chips over hot (not boiling) water; remove from heat.
ADD corn syrup and bourbon.
IN a large bowl, combine vanilla wafer crumbs, confectioners' sugar and nuts.
ADD chocolate mixture and mix well.
LET stand about 30 minutes.
FORM into 1-inch balls.
ROLL in granulated sugar.
LET season in covered container for several days.
YIELD: 4 1/2 dozen.

Chocolate-Covered Peanuts

1 pkg. chocolate pudding mix
1 c. sugar
1/2 c. top milk (use half &
   half)

1 1/2 c. salted peanuts
1 tsp. vanilla
1 T. butter

COOK pudding mix, sugar and milk 4 minutes; add other ingredients.
COOL and beat until stiff enough to drop by teaspoon on waxed paper.

Chocolate-Dipped Coffee Kisses

3 egg whites
1/4 tsp. cream of tartar
1 T. instant coffee granules
1 c. sugar
1/2 tsp. vanilla extract

1/2 c. chopped walnuts
3 (2 oz.) sq. chocolate candy
  coating, melted
1/2 c. finely-chopped walnuts,
  toasted

COMBINE the first 3 ingredients; beat at high speed with an electric mixer just until foamy.
ADD sugar, 1 tablespoon at a time, beating until stiff peaks form and sugar dissolves (2 to 4 minutes). Stir in vanilla and 1/2 cup walnuts. Drop by tablespoonfuls onto brown-paper-lined cookie sheets.
BAKE at 225° for 1 hour and 15 minutes. Turn oven "off", and leave cookies in oven 2 hours.
DIP bottom of each cookie in melted coating; dip again in toasted walnuts. Place on waxed paper until dry.
YIELD: 3 dozen.

Chocolate Peanut Brittle

2 c. sugar
1 c. light corn syrup
1/2 c. water
1 tsp. salt

6 oz. semi-sweet chocolate chips
2 T. butter
1 tsp. vanilla
1 1/2 c. salted peanuts

COMBINE sugar, syrup, water and salt; boil to hard-crack stage (300°) without stirring.
REMOVE from heat and quickly stir in chocolate chips, butter, vanilla and peanuts.
POUR quickly onto buttered cookie sheet.
WHEN cool, break into pieces.

Chocolate Truffle Cookies

4 sq. (1 oz. each) unsweetened chocolate
2 c. (12 oz.) semi-sweet chocolate chips, divided
1/3 c. butter or margarine
1 c. sugar
3 eggs
1 1/2 tsp. vanilla extract
1/2 c. all-purpose flour
2 T. baking cocoa
1/4 tsp. baking powder
1/4 tsp. salt
Confectioners' sugar

IN microwave or double boiler, melt unsweetened chocolate, 1 cup chocolate chips and butter; cool for 10 minutes.

IN a mixing bowl, beat sugar and eggs for 2 minutes.

BEAT in vanilla and the chocolate mixture.

COMBINE flour, cocoa, baking powder and salt; beat into chocolate mixture.

STIR in remaining chocolate chips.

COVER and chill for at least 3 hours.

REMOVE about 1 cup of dough.

WITH lightly-floured hands, roll into 1-inch balls.

PLACE on ungreased baking sheets.

BAKE at 350° for 10 to 12 minutes, or lightly puffed and set.

COOL on pan 3 to 4 minutes before removing to a wire rack to cool completely.

REPEAT with remaining dough.

DUST with confectioners' sugar.

YIELD: About 4 dozen.

Christmas Cookies

1 c. margarine
1 1/4 c. light brown sugar
3 eggs
3 c. flour
1 tsp. baking soda
1/2 tsp. salt
1 tsp. cinnamon
1/2 c. milk

3/4 lb. golden raisins
1 lb. candied cherries (red & green), chopped
6 slices candied pineapple (red & green), chopped
1 lb. dates, chopped
7 c. nuts, chopped

CREAM margarine and brown sugar; add eggs and beat until well blended.
COMBINE flour, baking soda, salt and cinnamon; blend with creamed mixture. Stir in remaining ingredients and blend well.
BAKE at 300° for 20 to 25 minutes.

Coconut and Pecan Candy

2 lb. powdered sugar
3 c. finely-chopped pecans
1 c. coconut
1 can Eagle Brand condensed milk

1 cube butter, melted (a cube of butter can be as little as 1/4 lb. or as much as 1/2 lb.)

SIFT powdered sugar, work all ingredients together and roll in small balls.
MELT 12 ounces chocolate chips with about 1/4 cup melted vegetable shortening and dip candy into this mixture for chocolate coating.

Cream Cheese Fudge

1 (3 oz.) pkg. cream cheese
1 lb. powdered sugar, sifted
3 to 6 T. water
1 c. chopped nuts (opt.)

1 to 2 tsp. vanilla
3 (1 oz.) sq. baking chocolate, melted

COMBINE cream cheese, sugar, water and vanilla until smooth.
BLEND in chocolate; add nuts if desired.
TURN into a buttered 9x13-inch buttered baking dish.
COOL and store in refrigerator.
CUT to desired size pieces, wrap in waxed paper. (You may make ahead and freeze.)

Candies and Cookies

Danish Kringlers

1 stick margarine	1 pt. cream
1 c. flour	4 c. flour
Pinch of baking soda or	
baking powder	

CUT margarine into the 1 cup flour.
ADD pinch of baking soda or baking powder.
STIR in cream and 4 cups flour.
ROLL in sugar.
CUT in strips 1/2-inch wide; form into bows.
DIP in sugar.
BAKE 10 to 15 minutes on ungreased cookie sheets.

Date-Nut Pinwheels

1 (8 oz.) pkg. pitted dates, chopped	2 c. firmly-packed brown sugar
1 c. sugar	2 eggs
1 c. hot water	1 tsp. vanilla extract
1 c. finely-chopped walnuts	3 1/2 c. all-purpose flour
1 c. butter or margarine, softened	1/2 tsp. baking soda
	1/2 tsp. cream of tartar
	1/2 tsp. salt

COMBINE dates, sugar and water in a medium saucepan; cook over medium heat, stirring constantly, about 6 to 8 minutes, or until mixture thickens.

REMOVE from heat; stir in walnuts and let cool completely.

CREAM butter in a large mixing bowl; gradually add brown sugar, beating well. Add eggs; beat well. Stir in vanilla.

COMBINE flour, baking soda, cream of tartar and salt in a medium bowl; add to creamed mixture, stirring well.

DIVIDE dough into thirds.

ROLL each portion into a 12-inch square on separate sheets of waxed paper; spread each square with 1/3 of reserved date mixture.

LIFTING up edge of waxed paper, gently peel off dough, and roll up jellyroll fashion, beginning with long end.

WRAP rolls in waxed paper, and chill overnight.

REMOVE waxed paper and cut into 1/4-inch slices, and place 2 inches apart on greased cookie sheets.

BAKE at 350° for 8 to 10 minutes.

REMOVE to wire racks to cool. Store in airtight containers.

YIELD: About 6 dozen.

English Toffee

1/2 lb. butter	1 T. vanilla
1 c. sugar	3 T. water

IN a heavy pan, cook over direct heat, stirring constantly.

AFTER it comes to a full boil, time it exactly 10 minutes.

POUR into buttered tins and put 5 small Hershey chocolate candy bars on top of hot candy.

AS the candy melts, spread out evenly over toffee.

French Vanilla Wafers

1/2 c. butter	1 tsp. vanilla
1/2 c. margarine	2 c. all-purpose flour
1 1/4 c. powdered sugar	1 tsp. baking soda
1 egg	1 tsp. cream of tartar
1/8 tsp. salt	

CREAM together butter and sugar.

BEAT in egg and vanilla.

COMBINE flour, baking soda, cream of tartar and salt; add to creamed mixture.

MIX well.

DIVIDE dough in half; form each half into 2-inch round roll.

WRAP in waxed paper or aluminum foil and chill in refrigerator or freezer (about 2 to 3 hours, or overnight in refrigerator).

SLICE 3/8-inch thick and place on an ungreased cookie sheet.

BAKE at 350° for 8 to 10 minutes.

THESE cookies are great plain, but may be iced accordingly to seasons.

Fudge

This is my own fudge recipe and different variations I have adapted to it, along with tips on problems that may occur during the cooking process.

Butter or margarine
2 c. sugar
3/4 c. milk
2 sq. (2 oz.) unsweetened
   chocolate
1 T. light corn syrup

Dash of salt
2 T. butter or margarine
1 tsp. vanilla
3/4 c. chopped candied fruit or
   dried fruit (opt.)
1/2 c. chopped nuts (opt.)

LIGHTLY grease the bottom and sides of an 8x8x2-inch pan with butter or margarine, or if thicker fudge is desired, 9x5x3-inch pan.

BUTTER the sides of a heavy 2-quart saucepan. Clip candy thermometer to side of pan.

IN the saucepan, combine sugar, milk, chocolate, corn syrup and salt. COOK and stir over medium heat until the sugar is dissolved and mixture begins to boil. Stir gently to avoid splashing syrup on the sides of pan, this causes the candy to become grainy.

THE mixture will begin to bubble vigorously and will rise close to the pan rim.

USE medium rather than high heat to prevent the mixture from sticking or boiling over.

CONTINUE cooking the mixture, stirring only as necessary to prevent sticking, to 234° or the soft-ball stage (a few drops of the mixture, dropped from a teaspoon into cold water, form a soft ball that flattens when removed from the water). (Be sure to watch closely; the temperature rises very quickly above 220°.)

IMMEDIATELY remove pan from heat; add the 2 tablespoons butter or margarine, but <u>do not stir</u>. Cool mixture, without stirring or moving pan, until thermometer registers 100°, or until the bottom of the pan feels comfortably warm to the touch. Stirring or moving the mixture can result in coarse, grainy candy.

Continued on following page.

        Candies and Cookies

Continued from preceding page.

REMOVE the thermometer. Stir in vanilla; beat mixture by hand with a wooden spoon, lifting candy with an up-and-over motion, until mixture becomes thick, starts to lose its gloss, and doesn't stream back into the pan when the spoon is lifted (or until a small amount of the mixture holds its shape when dropped onto waxed paper). Do not use an electric mixer.

IMMEDIATELY stir in fruit and nuts, if desired. Quickly pour mixutre into prepared pan.

DO NOT scrape pan, the sides will have a less creamy mixture.

DECORATE with additional chopped nuts or nut halves, if desired.

SCORE lightly in squares with a sharp knife; cool.

CUT into squares. Store tightly covered in a cool place.

DO not chill in refrigerator.

YIELD: 1 1/4 pounds.

Fudge-Making Tips

BE sure that all of the sugar in the boiling mixture is completely dissolved. Any undissolved sugar will give the fudge an undesirable grainy texture.

USE an accurate candy thermometer for best results.

WHEN cooling the fudge to 110°, let the mixture stand undisturbed. At this stage, the mixture is very sensitive to moving, jarring or stirring, which can make the candy coarse and grainy.

A wooden spoon is the ideal tool for beating fudge - do not use a mixer, as the mixture will overtax the mixer motor. Beat vigorously by hand with an up-and-over motion.

CHECK the consistency of the fudge frequently during beating. As soon as the mixture feels thick, lift the spoon out. If the fudge "hangs" from the spoon without streaming back into the pan, it's ready to pour out.

IF you've beaten the fudge too long, you won't be able to pour it out. Scrape it out of the pan and knead it with your fingers. Shape it into a log, or roll into 1-inch balls.

IF fudge doesn't set, stir in an additional 1/4 cup cold milk, and repeat steps 2 and 3, and 4 of the recipe. Do not add more butter or vanilla.

NEVER try to double the recipe - the candy will not cook properly and beating the mixture will be difficult.

Candies and Cookies

Fudge - Shaping

BALLS - Shape fudge into 1-inch balls; while warm, roll in finely-chopped nuts, grated coconut or crushed peppermint candies.

MOLDED - Oil small individual molds; press fudge into molds. Unmold, using wooden toothpicks to loosen corners; allow candies to set on waxed paper.

CUT-OUTS - Spread fudge 1/2-inch-thick on a buttered cookie sheet or waxed paper; cut into shapes with small canape or cookie cutters.

RING - Generously butter a 2-cup ring mold; sprinkle with 3 table-spoons chopped nuts or finely-crushed peppermint candies. Turn fudge into mold; cool. Loosen sides with a narrow metal spatula. Unmold onto plate; slice.

LOG - Shape fudge into log with buttered fingers; roll in chopped nuts, coconut or crushed peppermint candies. Cool; cut into 3/8-inch-thick slices.

Fudge Variations

It is always fun making the different variations - every family member will have their own favorite.

COFFEE PENUCHE:
PREPARE original fudge recipe, except: reduce granulated sugar to 1 1/2 cups, add 1 cup packed brown sugar and 1 tablespoon instant coffee crystals with the granulated sugar.
OMIT the chocolate, and the fruit and nut options.
SPREAD beaten mixture in a buttered 9x5x3-inch loaf pan; sprinkle 1/2 cup toasted, sliced almonds on top of warm candy; press in lightly with your hands.
COOL; cut into squares.
STORE tightly covered.
YIELD: 40 pieces.

FOUR-LAYER MINT FUDGE:
PREPARE the original fudge recipe, omitting the fruit and nut options.
WHILE fudge is cooling to 100°, prepare mint layer: In a small mixing bowl, beat 1/4 cup butter or margarine on high speed of an electric mixer until fluffy. Gradually beat in 2 1/4 cups sifted powdered sugar alternately with 2 tablespoons green creme de menthe; beat until smooth. Cover and set aside.
POUR beaten fudge onto a square of foil or waxed paper.
WITH a buttered rolling pin, quickly roll fudge to a 12x10-inch rectangle.
WHEN fudge begins to set, spread half of the mint mixture evenly over half of the fudge.
USING foil or paper to lift fudge, invert plain fudge over mint-covered fudge; carefully peel off foil or paper.
SPREAD remaining mint mixture over top fudge layer.
REFRIGERATE until firm; cut into 2 x 1/2-inch sticks with a sharp knife.
STORE tightly covered in a cool place.
YIELD: About 1 3/4 pounds.

Continued on following page.

Continued from preceding page.

GERMAN CHOCOLATE FUDGE:
BUTTER a 9x5x3-inch loaf pan. Prepare original fudge recipe except, decrease sugar to 1 3/4 cups, substitute 3 squares (3 ounces) sweet chocolate for the unsweetened chocolate, use pecans for the nuts and omit the fruit option.
POUR the beaten fudge in loaf pan; sprinkle 1/3 cup toasted coconut evenly on top, pressing gently with your hands.
SCORE, cut into squares when cool.
STORE candy tightly covered in a cool place.
YIELD: About 40 pieces.

PEANUT BUTTER MARBLE FUDGE:
PREPARE original fudge recipe, omitting the fruit and nut options. When fudge becomes thick during beating, add 3/4 cup peanut butter; swirl once or twice to marble.
IMMEDIATELY spread fudge in the buttered pan. Cool; cut into squares.
STORE candy tightly covered in a cool place.
YIELD: 40 pieces.

FUDGE S'MORES:
PLACE 9 graham crackers in the bottom of a foil-lined 8x8x2-inch pan, cutting crackers to fit, if necessary.
SPRINKLE with 1 cup miniature marshmallows.
PREPARE original fudge recipe, omitting fruit and nut options, and quickly pour beaten fudge evenly over marshmallows, spreading to cover completely.
SPRINKLE 1/2 cup chopped walnuts on top, pressing in with your hands.
SCORE; cool and cut into squares.
STORE tightly covered in a cool place.
YIELD: 36 pieces.

Continued on following page.

Continued from preceding page.

FUDGE-ALMOND BON BONS:
BUTTER a 9x5x3-inch loaf pan.
PREPARE original fudge recipe, except: use 1 teaspoon vanilla or 1/2 teaspoon almond extract, and omit the fruit and nut options.
POUR beaten fudge in pan; score into squares and cool. Once cool, cut squares.
IN double boiler over hot, not boiling water, melt 1 pound white chocolate. (You will find in grocery, as white chocolate bark.)
FOR each bon bon, hold 1 square at a time on a fork over melted white chocolate; spoon melted white chocolate over fudge piece, covering all sides.
PLACE candy pieces on waxed paper or foil; top each piece with a whole unblanched almond.
ALLOW pieces to dry; store in a covered container between layers of waxed paper.
STORE in a cool place.
YIELD: About 32 pieces.

German Apple Cake

This is a recipe from my husband's grandmother, Frieda Hoffmann. Grandma was a truly great cook and a wonderful and loving person.

2 eggs	2 c. flour
2 scant c. sugar	1 tsp. baking soda
4 c. apples, diced	1 tsp. cinnamon
1 c. oil	1/2 tsp. salt
1/2 c. nuts	1 tsp. vanilla

PUT all ingredients together and don't stir too much.
MIX together 3/4 cup brown sugar and 1/2 cup chopped nuts, and cover top of batter before baking.
BAKE at 350° for 40 to 50 minutes in a greased 9x13-inch pan.
SERVE with whipped cream or ice cream.

Ginger Cookies

1/2 c. shortening	2 tsp. baking soda
2 c. sugar	1 tsp. ground cinnamon
2 lg. eggs	1 tsp. ground cloves
1/2 c. molasses	1 tsp. ginger
4 c. all-purpose flour	Sugar

COMBINE the first 9 ingredients in a large mixing bowl; beat at medium speed with an electric mixer until mixture is blended. SHAPE into 1-inch balls, and roll in additional sugar. Place on greased cookie sheets, and flatten slightly with a flat-bottomed glass. BAKE at 375° for 8 to 10 minutes. Transfer to wire racks to cool. YIELD: 7 dozen.

Grandma Jakoby's Cinnamon Stars

German Recipe. This recipe is from Lois Jakoby, our master gardener, whose monthly gardening tips were in our planting and pickling cookbook. This recipe is from Frances Poppe Jakoby (1881-1947). She always made these for Christmas. Lois says "sometimes to dry the cut cookies and grind the nuts takes extra time, but - it's tradition!

1 c. sugar	1 1/4 tsp. salt
1 tsp. cinnamon	1 1/2 c. unroasted peanuts, finely
1 tsp. grated lemon rind	chopped or ground
3 egg whites	

COMBINE the first 3 ingredients.
BEAT egg whites and salt until stiff peaks.
ADD sugar gradually, beating constantly.
CONTINUE to beat until thick and holds shape.
SET aside 1/2 cup for frosting.
STIR in nuts. Chill well.
ROLL out in small amounts 1/2-inch thick, using generous amounts of confectioners' sugar on board.
CUT with a star cutter.
TOP with a small amount of reserved frosting.
PLACE on greased cookie sheets to dry overnight.
BAKE at 300° for 25 minutes.

Hermits

4 c. sifted flour	2 c. brown sugar
1 tsp. baking soda	4 eggs
1 tsp. nutmeg	1/4 c. milk
1/2 tsp. cinnamon	2 c. raisins
1/2 tsp. salt	1 c. chopped walnuts
1 c. butter or margarine	

SIFT together flour, baking soda, nutmeg, cinnamon and salt; set aside.
IN a large mixing bowl, beat at medium speed of an electric mixer, butter and brown sugar.
ADD eggs, one at a time, beating well after each addition.
GRADUALLY beat in flour mixture alternately with milk.
STIR in raisins and walnuts.
REFRIGERATE, covered, until well chilled (about 3 hours).
DROP by spoonfuls about 2 inches apart, on greased cookie sheets.
BAKE in preheated 375° oven 15 minutes, or until golden.
ICE, if you prefer. You may make them very festive with colored icing.

Holiday Quick Pudding

This is a recipe from my mother-in-law, Ione Schneckloth, she always makes the holidays a very special treat for all of us. As well as being one of the most wonderful cooks I know, she is very talented, and has the most beautiful Christmas decorations you will ever see.

1 c. flour + 1/4 tsp. salt	1/2 c. raisins
1 c. sugar	1/2 c. nuts
1/2 c. milk	1/2 c. chopped dates

MIX sugar, raisins, nuts and chopped dates together with flour.
ADD milk.
SPREAD mixutre in a flat 9x13-inch greased baking pan.

TOPPING:	2 T. butter
1 c. brown sugar	2 c. boiling water

MIX topping together and pour over ingredients in pan.
BAKE at 350° until crust on top is brown, 20 to 25 minutes.
SERVE with whipped cream.

Candies and Cookies

Holly Christmas Cookie

1 c. butter or margarine,
   softened
1/4 c. butter-flavored
   shortening
1 c. sugar
2 lg. eggs
4 c. all-purpose flour

2 tsp. grated orange rind
1 egg white
2 T. sugar
Red candied cherries, cut into
   fourths
Chopped green citron

BEAT butter and shortening at medium speed with an electric mixer until creamy; gradually add 1 cup sugar, beating well.

ADD eggs, one at a time, beating until blended after each addition. Gradually add flour and orange rind, beating mixture at low speed after each addition.

DIVIDE dough into 4 portions; shape each portion into a ball and wrap in plastic wrap; chill 2 hours.

REMOVE 1 ball of dough from refrigerator; divide dough into 18 portions. Roll each portion into a 6-inch rope. Loop each rope into a circle, crossing ends to resemble an "X"; place on ungreased cookie sheets.

BEAT egg whites at high speed until foamy; gradually add 2 tablespoons sugar, beating until stiff peaks form and sugar dissolves.

BRUSH egg white mixture over tops of cookies; arrange cherries and citron where dough overlaps to resemble holly, and lightly press into dough.

BAKE at 400° for 10 minutes, or until golden (do not brown). Let stand on cookie sheets 5 minutes; transfer to wire racks to cool completely. Repeat with remaining dough.

YIELD: 6 dozen.

Inez Cookies

1 c. butter (must be butter)
3/4 c. butter
2 1/2 c. sifted all-purpose
    flour

1 c. ground walnuts or pecans
1 1/2 tsp. vanilla

COMBINE all ingredients thoroughly.
KNEAD to a smooth dough.
ROLL about a teaspoon of dough into a ball, flatten with tines of a fork.
PLACE on an ungreased cookie sheet.
BAKE at 350° until slightly browned, about 15 to 17 minutes (do not overbrown).
ROLL cookies in granulated sugar while still warm (take care, as they are delicate).
YIELD: About 3 to 4 dozen cookies.

Lemon-Walnut Fudge

3 oz. cream cheese
1 tsp. grated lemon peel
1 T. lemon juice

4 c. powdered sugar
1/2 c. chopped walnuts

CREAM cheese until soft.
ADD lemon peel and juice gradually; blend well.
ADD sugar gradually; stir in nuts.
PRESS into a greased 9x5-inch pan and chill until firm.
YIELD: 18 large pieces.

Mamie Eisenhower's Fudge

4 1/2 c. sugar
1/4 tsp. salt
2 T. butter
1 lg. can evaporated milk

12 oz. sweet German chocolate
12 oz. semi-sweet chocolate bits
1 pt. marshmallow creme
2 c. nutmeats

COMBINE sugar, salt, butter and evaporated milk in a large saucepan; bring to a rolling boil.
BOIL for 6 minutes.
MIX remaining ingredients in a large mixing bowl and beat until all chocolate is thoroughly melted and candy is smooth.
LET stand in buttered pan until cool and set.

Marshmallow Creme Divinity

COOK 1 1/2 cups sugar, 1/3 cup water and a pinch of salt to the hard ball stage. Do not overcook. Beat syrup into a pint of marshmallow creme and 1 teaspoon vanilla, along with 1/2 cup nuts. Drop by teaspoonful on waxed paper to set.
FOR DIVINITY LOGS: Shape divinity into rolls about 6 inches long. Place on cookie sheet and freeze until hard. Mix 1 can Eagle Brand condensed milk with 1 cup light corn syrup. Cook over medium heat, stirring constantly, to soft ball stage and mixture turns caramel color. Remove from heat. Place chopped nuts on cookie sheet. Roll divinity in caramel, then in chopped nuts. Let cool and slice.

Mexican Wedding Cookies

Always a favorite.

1 c. pecans or walnuts
2/3 c. powdered sugar
1 c. butter or margarine,
    softened

1 tsp. vanilla
1 3/4 c. all-purpose flour

PREHEAT oven to 350°.
IN food processor or blender, process nuts with 2 tablespoons powdered sugar until finely ground; set aside.
IN a large bowl, beat butter and remaining sugar.
BEAT in vanilla and add flour and nut mixture; mix until well blended.
ROLL in powdered sugar.
PLACE 2 inches apart on an ungreased cookie sheet.
BAKE 10 to 12 minutes, or until just golden around edges.
REMOVE from oven and again roll in powdered sugar. Allow to cool.
YIELD: 2 to 3 dozen.

Mint Meringue Kisses

2 egg whites (lg. eggs)
Pinch of salt
1/2 tsp. cream of tartar
3/4 c. granulated sugar

6 oz. mint-flavored chocolate
    chips
Green food coloring

PREHEAT oven to 375°.
WHIP egg whites until stiff; add salt and cream of tartar. Add sugar gradually.
STIR in chips and several drops of food coloring.
DROP by teaspoon on lightly-greased cookie sheets (will make 2 full sheets). Turn off oven.
PLACE cookies in oven and leave overnight.
YIELD: 3 dozen cookies.

Candies and Cookies

Molasses Cookies

This is another recipe from Evelyn Rupple from Medina, Wisconsin.

1 c. shortening, melted	2 tsp. baking soda
2/3 c. molasses	1 tsp. ginger
1 c. sugar	2 tsp. cinnamon
2 eggs	1 tsp. salt
3 1/2 c. flour	

SIFT together flour, baking soda, ginger, cinnamon and salt; set aside.
CREAM together shortening, sugar and molasses.
COMBINE the reserved flour mixture and the creamed mixture; mix well.
DROP by small tablespoonfuls onto a greased cookie sheet.
BAKE at 350° for 12 to 15 minutes.
REMOVE from oven, and frost immediately with a powdered sugar glaze, made with 2 cups of powdered sugar; add water to desired thickness. You may use any icing of your choice, or sprinkle with granulated sugar.
YIELD: 2 to 2 1/2 dozen cookies.

Mrs. Campbell's Sugar Cookies

This recipe was given to my mother many years ago by one of my friends' mother. We were told that it was her mother's recipe handed down from ancestors in Scotland. We have always enjoyed them so much, we never make any other sugar cookie. It is extremely easy to make, and easy to handle when cutting your shapes for the holidays.

1 c. sugar	4 c. flour (do not sift)
2 c. butter (never use margarine)	

MIX all ingredients together and chill about 15 minutes.
ROLL out and cut into desired shapes.
BAKE at 325° until set, about 8 to 10 minutes (watch carefully).
FROST, if desired.
YIELD: 5 to 7 dozen.

Neopolitan Cookies

1 c. butter or margarine, softened	1/2 tsp. salt
1 1/2 c. sugar	1/2 tsp. almond extract
1 egg	Red food coloring
1 tsp. vanilla extract	1/2 c. chopped pecans or walnuts
2 1/2 c. all-purpose flour	1 (1 oz.) sq. unsweetened
1 1/2 tsp. baking powder	chocolate, melted

LINE bottom and sides of a 9x5x3-inch loaf pan with waxed paper.

CREAM butter in a large mixing bowl; gradually add sugar, beating until light and fluffy.

ADD egg; beat well and stir in vanilla.

COMBINE flour, baking powder and salt in a medium mixing bowl; add to creamed mixture, beating just until blended.

DIVIDE dough into thirds.

ADD almond extract and 5 drops red food coloring to one portion; spread mixture evenly in prepared pan.

ADD pecans to second portion; spread mixture evenly over dough in pan.

ADD melted chocolate to remaining portion; spread mixture evenly over dough in pan. Cover and refrigerate overnight.

TURN dough out of pan, and remove waxed paper.

CUT dough in half lengthwise; cut each half crosswise into 1/8-inch slices.

PLACE 1-inch apart on ungreased cookie sheets.

BAKE at 350° for 10 to 12 minutes.

REMOVE to wire racks to cool.

STORE in airtight containers.

YIELD: 5 dozen.

Candies and Cookies

New England Gingersnaps

3/4 c. butter or margarine	2 tsp. baking soda
1 c. sugar	1 tsp. ginger
1 egg	1 tsp. cinnamon
1/4 c. molasses	1 tsp. ground cloves
2 c. all-purpose flour	Additional sugar

CREAM butter in a large mixing bowl; gradually add 1 cup sugar, beating until light and fluffy.

ADD egg and molasses; beat well.

SIFT together flour, baking soda and spices.

ADD to creamed mixture, beating until smooth; chill 2 hours.

SHAPE dough into 3/4-inch balls, and roll in additional sugar to coat well.

PLACE 2 inches apart on greased cookie sheets.

BAKE at 350° for 11 to 12 minutes. (Cookies will puff up and then flatten.)

COOL slightly on cookie sheets; remove to wire racks to cool completely.

YIELD: about 6 dozen.

Nougat

2 c. sugar	2 egg whites
1 1/3 c. white Karo syrup	3 oz. honey
1/2 c. water	

BOIL sugar, syrup and water to 285°, or to the soft crack stage.

BEAT 2 egg whites; when whites start to stand up, add honey slowly, by hand, beating constantly until thick.

ADD almond extract or nuts if desired.

Oatmeal Cookies

This cookie recipe is from my husband's grandmother, Nora Lensch Schneckloth, she was a wonderful person and a great cook. She always made sure that you never, never left her house hungry and well loved.

1 c. sugar	1/2 tsp. cloves
1 3/4 c. shortening	1/2 tsp. nutmeg
3 eggs	1 tsp. salt
2 c. rolled oats* (quick cook)	1 tsp. vanilla
1 c. raisins	1 tsp. baking soda
1 c. nuts, chopped	2 tsp. baking powder
1/2 c. dates, finely chopped	2 c. flour
1 tsp. cinnamon	

MIX together flour, baking soda, baking powder, salt and spices; set aside.

CREAM together sugar, shortening and eggs; fold in raisins, dates, nuts and oats; mix well.

COMBINE flour mixture and creamed mixture, blending well.

BAKE at 350° for 12 to 15 minutes, or until set. (It is a good idea to bake a test cookie to see if you have enough flour.)

*You may replace the 2 cups of oats with 1 cup oats and 1 1/2 cups Rice Krispies or Wheaties.

Opamodies

This recipe with the strange name is another from our master gardener, Lois Jakoby. Lois doesn't seem to remember where the name originated, but they have always been called Opamodies. Lois says "We suspect it came from our Chrissy, who also named a Bushy Bushy Congo Cake. It was a popular treat because the girls could make them after their 12th birthday." I made this recipe with the strange name and strange name or not, it is delicious!

2 c. sugar	1 tsp. vanilla
1 stick margarine	1 c. peanut butter
1/2 c. milk	3 c. oatmeal
4 T. cocoa	

COMBINE the first 4 ingredients in a saucepan and bring to a boil.
REMOVE from heat; add vanilla and quickly stir in peanut butter, then oats.
DROP by teaspoonfuls onto waxed paper.

Peanut Blossoms

1/2 c. butter	1 3/4 c. all-purpose flour
1/3 c. peanut butter	1 tsp baking soda
1/2 c. sugar	1/2 tsp. salt
1/2 c. packed brown sugar	1/2 c. granulated sugar
1 unbeaten egg	Milk chocolate candy kisses
1 tsp. vanilla	

SIFT together dry ingredients and set aside.
CREAM together butter, peanut butter, sugar and brown sugar; add unbeaten egg and vanilla.
BEAT well; add dry ingredients gradually and mix thoroughly.
SHAPE dough into balls, using a rounded teaspoonful for each.
ROLL balls in sugar and place on greased cookie sheet.
BAKE at 375° for 8 minutes.
REMOVE from oven; top each cookie with a solid milk chocolate candy kiss, pressing down firmly so cookie cracks around edge.
RETURN to oven; bake 2 to 5 minutes longer until golden brown.
YIELD: 3 dozen cookies.

Peanut Brittle

1 c. sugar	1 tsp. butter
1/2 c. white corn syrup	1 tsp. vanilla
1 c. peanuts (roasted, salted)	1 tsp. baking soda

PLACE sugar and corn syrup in a 1/2-quart casserole dish; stir together and microwave 4 minutes.
STIR in peanuts and cook 3 to 5 minutes until light brown.
STIR in butter and vanilla; cook 1 1/2 to 2 minutes.
ADD baking soda and stir until light and foamy.
POUR mixture onto a lightly-greased cookie sheet.
BAKE at 300° for 1/2 to 1 hour.
BREAK into small pieces and store in an airtight container.
YIELD: 1 pound.

Peanut Butter Balls

3/4 c. mashed potatoes	1 c. peanut butter
1 lb. confectioners' sugar	Chocolate chips

BOIL potatoes until well done.
MASH and add sugar until thick and smooth; add peanut butter and stir.
ROLL in balls and dip in melted chocolate. (You may use chocolate chips, about 1 small bag with 1/2 tablespoon shortening, or chocolate such as Wiltons. I melt the chocolate in the microwave.)
PLACE on waxed paper for 10 minutes.
STORE in refrigerator.
YIELD: About 25 to 30 minutes.

Candies and Cookies

Peanut Butter Fudge

2 c. sugar	1/2 c. peanut butter (creamy or
1/2 c. evaporated milk	chunky)
1/2 c. corn syrup	1 tsp. vanilla
Pinch of salt	1 T. margarine

ON medium heat, combine sugar, milk, corn syrup and salt; bring to a boil until sugar is almost melted.

ADD peanut butter; boil until medium soft ball stage.

REMOVE from heat.

ADD vanilla and margarine; let stand until margarine melts.

BEAT with a wooden spoon until it just begins to lose its gloss.

POUR into a buttered 8x8-inch pan.

COOL slightly; score. Cool completely and cut.

YIELD: 24 (1-inch) pieces.

Peanut Clusters

2 c. sugar	1 heaping T. butter
1 T. cocoa	1 c. salted peanuts
1/2 c. milk	1 tsp. vanilla

COMBINE sugar, cocoa and sweet milk; boil 6 minutes after boiling point is reached.

ADD butter, peanuts and vanilla.

STIR well and drop on waxed paper.

Pecan Fudge

3 c. white sugar	1 1/2 c. milk
1/2 c. light corn syrup	1 c. pecans
2 c. brown sugar	

COOK to soft-boil stage, 232° on the candy thermometer; cool.

BEAT; and before stiff, add pecans.

POUR into buttered pan.

Pfeffernuesse Fruit Cake Cookies

1/2 c. sugar	1/4 tsp. nutmeg
1/2 c. shortening	1/2 c. candied cherries, chopped
1/2 c. dark corn syrup	1/2 c. raisins
1/2 c. coffee	1/2 c. dates
3 1/4 c. flour	1/2 c. walnuts
1/2 tsp. cinnamon	2 unbeaten eggs
1 1/2 tsp. baking soda	1/2 tsp. anise extract
1/4 tsp. salt	1 tsp. anise seed

COMBINE sugar, shortening, dark corn syrup and coffee in a sauce-pan and simmer 5 minutes; cool.

SIFT flour, cinnamon, baking soda, salt and nutmeg together.

GRIND cherries, raisins, dates and walnuts. (You may use your food processor.)

MIX the ground ingredients into the sifted dry ingredients.

ADD the eggs and then the sugar mixture; stir well.

CHILL 4 hours, or overnight.

SHAPE into balls with well-floured hands.

BAKE on greased cookie sheet at 350° for 15 to 18 minutes.

DIP warm cookies in a glaze made of 1/2 cup water, 1/4 teaspoon cream of tartar, and 1 cup sugar, boiled until clear.

COOL cookies after dipped in glaze.

STORE in tight container.

Pineapple Fudge

5 1/2 c. sugar	1/2 c. white corn syrup
1 c. crushed pineapple, drained	A lg. lump of butter
1 c. cream	Juice of 1 lemon

COMBINE sugar, pineapple, cream, corn syrup and butter; cook to soft ball stage.

SET aside to cool.

WHEN cool enough to handle with your hands, beat it until it looks grainy.

ADD lemon juice and nuts; pour into a buttered pan.

CUT into squares when set.

Pralines

2 c. light brown sugar
1 c. granulated sugar
1 sm. can evaporated milk
2 T. Karo syrup

2 tsp. vanilla
1 stick butter
1 c. chopped pecans

MELT butter over medium heat.
BLEND together milk and syrup (blend well or milk will curdle).
STIR in mixed brown sugar and white sugar and vanilla.
REMOVE from heat; add pecans.
DROP on waxed paper, a small amount and let cool. (I usually try to make each praline about 1 1/2-inch diameter, about a generous teaspoon.)
YIELD: About 25 pralines.

Pumpkin Spice Cookies

1/2 c. shortening	1 tsp. ground cinnamon
1 1/2 c. sugar	1 tsp. ground nutmeg
2 eggs	1/2 tsp. ground allspice
1 c. mashed, cooked	1/4 tsp. ground ginger
pumpkin	1 tsp. salt
1 tsp. vanilla extract	1 T. baking powder
1/2 tsp. lemon extract	1 c. raisins
1 tsp. grated lemon rind	1/2 c. chopped pecans
2 1/2 c. all-purpose flour	Lemon Buttercream Frosting (opt.)

CREAM shortening in a large mixing bowl; gradually add sugar, beating well.
ADD eggs, beat until well blended.
STIR in pumpkin, vanilla, lemon extract and grated lemon rind.
COMBINE flour, baking powder, salt and spices in a medium mixing bowl; stir well.
GRADUALLY add to creamed mixture, stirring well.
STIR in raisins and pecans.
DROP dough by teaspoonfuls, 2 inches apart, onto greased cookie sheets.
BAKE at 375° for 12 minutes, or until lightly browned.
REMOVE to wire racks to cool.
FROST with Lemon Buttercream Frosting, if desired.
YIELD: 7 dozen cookies.

LEMON BUTTERCREAM FROSTING:

1/4 c. butter, softened	3 T. half & half
2 1/4 c. sifted powdered	1/2 tsp. grated lemon rind
sugar, divided	

CREAM butter in medium mixing bowl; gradually add 1 cup powdered sugar, beating until well blended.
ADD remaining powdered sugar alternately with half & half, beating until smooth.
ADD lemon rind, and beat well.
YIELD: Frosting for 7 dozen cookies.

Candies and Cookies

Sand Tarts

1 c. butter or margarine	2 tsp. vanilla extract
2 c. sugar	4 c. all-purpose flour
2 eggs	Cinnamon
1 egg, separated	Additional sugar

CREAM butter in a large mixing bowl; gradually add 2 cups sugar, beating well.

ADD eggs and egg yolk; beat well. Stir in vanilla.

ADD flour; mix well.

ROLL to 1/4-inch thickness on a lightly-floured surface.

CUT with a 2 1/2-inch round cutter.

BEAT egg white lightly; brush over cookies.

COMBINE cinnamon and additional sugar; sprinkle over cookies.

PLACE 2 inches apart on greased cookie sheets.

BAKE at 350° for 8 to 10 minutes.

YIELD: About 6 dozen.

Swedish Yule Cookies

6 eggs, separated	3/4 c. shortening
2 c. sifted flour	3/4 c. sugar
1/2 tsp. salt	1 tsp. lemon extract

DROP yolks one at a time into hot salted water and simmer until hard-cooked.

SIFT flour and salt together.

ADD sugar to shortening gradually, beating until light and fluffy.

PUT cooked yolks through a sieve and add to creamed mixture, along with lemon extract.

BLEND cream, alternately with dry ingredients, into mixture.

BEAT well after each addition.

ROLL dough 1/8-inch thick and cut in different shapes appropriate for the holidays.

DOUGH may be used in a cookie press, or shaped into knots by rolling small on lightly-floured board until about 6 inches in length, and tied in a loose knot.

DECORATE cookies with colored sugar, candied fruit, coconut and nuts.

BAKE in 375° oven until edges show a delicate brown.

ALLOW 6 to 8 minutes for rolled or pressed cookies and 10 to 12 minutes for knots.

Candies and Cookies   **215**

Swiss Almond Christmas Wafers

1 1/2 c. lightly-toasted
  sliced almonds
1/2 c. sugar
2 tsp. grated orange rind
1/2 c. butter or margarine,
  softened
1 egg
2 egg yolks

2 T. amaretto
2 1/4 c. all-purpose flour
1/4 tsp. salt
1 egg yolk
1 T. water
Additional sugar, colored sugar,
  or decorations for top of
  cookie of choice

COMBINE almonds, 1/2 cup sugar and orange rind in container of a food processor or electric blender; process until almonds are finely ground.
CREAM butter in a large mixing bowl, beating until well blended.
ADD almond mixture, beating well.
ADD egg, 2 egg yolks and amaretto; beat until light and fluffy.
COMBINE flour and salt in a medium mixing bowl; add to creamed mixture and mix until well blended.
SHAPE dough into a ball; wrap in waxed paper and chill until firm.
ROLL dough to 1/4-inch thickness between 2 sheets of waxed paper. (Turn dough over frequently to allow dough to spread.)
CUT with a 2-inch round cutter, rerolling scraps of dough.
PLACE 1/2-inch apart on greased and floured cookie sheets.
COMBINE 1 egg yolk and water in a small mixing bowl, blending well; brush mixture evenly over tops of cookies.
SPRINKLE additional sugar lightly over cookies and decorate as desired.
BAKE at 350° for 15 to 18 minutes, or until browned around edges.
REMOVE to wire racks to cool; store in airtight containers.
YIELD: 5 1/2 dozen cookies.

Candies and Cookies

Thumbprint-Icing Cookies

3/4 c. butter	1 1/2 c. sifted all-purpose flour
1/2 c. firmly-packed brown sugar	1/4 tsp. salt
1 unbeaten egg yolk	1 c. finely-chopped pecans
1/2 tsp. vanilla	Confectioners' icing for centers (*see recipe below)

SIFT together flour and salt; set aside.

CREAM together butter, brown sugar, egg yolk and vanilla.

ADD dry ingredients; mix thoroughly and chill 1 hour for easier handling.

SHAPE dough into balls, 1-inch in diameter.

DIP into slightly beaten egg white, then into chopped pecans.

PLACE on ungreased baking sheet.

PRESS deep hole in center of cookie with floured thimble or finger.

BAKE at 375° for 12 to 15 minutes.

YIELD: 3 dozen cookies.

CONFECTIONERS' SUGAR:

3/4 c. sifted confectioners' sugar	1 T. soft butter
	1 T. cream cheese

MIX all ingredients together and blend until smooth. (You may add heavy cream if too stiff, until correct consistency). You may add whichever color to the frosting you desire.

PLACE about l/2 teaspoon icing in the hollow of each cookie.

LET stand until set, and store in a flat container.

Notes &
Recipes

Candies and Cookies

INGREDIENT SUBSTITUTIONS
AND EQUIVALENTS

List Your Favorite Recipes

Recipes   **Page**

_____   _____

_____   _____

_____   _____

_____   _____

_____   _____

_____   _____

_____   _____

_____   _____

_____   _____

_____   _____

_____   _____

_____   _____

_____   _____

_____   _____

_____   _____

_____   _____

RECIPE INGREDIENTS	SUBSTITUTIONS
1 cup sour milk or buttermilk	1 tablespoon vinegar or lemon juice plus sweet milk to make 1 cup
1 cup commercial sour cream	1 tablespoon lemon juice plus evaporated milk to equal 1 cup
1 cup yogurt	1 cup sour milk or buttermilk
1 whole egg	2 egg whites or 1/4 cup egg substitute
1 tablespoon cornstarch	2 tablespoons all-purpose flour
1 teaspoon baking powder	1/2 teaspoon cream of tartar plus 1/4 teaspoon baking soda
1 cup cake flour	1 cup all-purpose flour minus 2 tablespoons
1 cup self-rising flour	1 cup all-purpose flour plus 1 teaspoon baking powder and 1/2 teaspoon salt
1 cup honey	1 1/4 cups sugar plus 1/4 cup liquid
1 ounce unsweetened chocolate	3 tablespoons cocoa plus 1 tablespoon butter or margarine
1 pound fresh mushrooms	6 ounces canned mushrooms
1 tablespoon fresh herbs	1 teaspoon ground or crushed dry herbs
1 teaspoon onion powder	2 teaspoons minced onion
1 clove fresh garlic	1 teaspoon garlic salt or 1/8 teaspoon garlic powder
Dry sherry	Dry vermouth
1 cup cream	1 cup skim milk plus 2 tablespoons nonfat dry milk; or 3/4 cup milk plus 1/3 cup butter

Ingredient Substitutions and Equivalents　　　219

EQUIVALENT MEASURES

3 teaspoons	1 tablespoon
4 tablespoons	1/4 cup
5 1/3 tablespoons	1/3 cup
8 tablespoons	1/2 cup
16 tablespoons	1 cup
2 tablespoons	1 ounce (liquid)
1 cup	8 fluid ounces
1/2 cup	4 fluid ounces
1 pound	16 ounces
2 cups	1 pint (16 fluid oz.)
4 cups	1 quart
4 quarts	1 gallon
1/8 cup	2 tablespoons
1/3 cup	5 tablespoons + 1 tsp.
2/3 cup	10 tablespoons + 2 tsp.
3/4 cup	12 tablespoons
2 cups fat	1 pound

MEASUREMENT CONVERSION FORMULAS

HOW TO CONVERT:

liters x 2.12 = pints	kilograms x 2.21 = pounds
liters x 1.06 = quarts	grams x .035 = ounces
pints x .472 = liters	pounds x .45 = kilograms
quarts x .946 = liters	ounces x 28.35 = grams

TEMPERATURES

250° Fahrenheit	= 121° Celsius
300° Fahrenheit	= 149° Celsius
350° Fahrenheit	= 177° Celsius
400° Fahrenheit	= 205° Celsius
450° Fahrenheit	= 232° Celsius

Ingredient Substitutions and Equivalents

ORDER BLANK

NAME _____

ADDRESS _____

CITY & STATE _____ ZIP _____

How many copies? _____ Amount enclosed _____
    Price per book $12.00
    Postage & handling 2.50
    Total $14.50
Please make checks payable to:
                 The Machine Shed
Mail orders to: Country Holiday Favorites
                 111 W. 76th Street
                 Davenport, IA 52806

- -

ORDER BLANK

NAME _____

ADDRESS _____

CITY & STATE _____ ZIP _____

How many copies? _____ Amount enclosed _____
    Price per book $12.00
    Postage & handling 2.50
    Total $14.50
Please make checks payable to:
                 The Machine Shed
Mail orders to: Country Holiday Favorites
                 111 W. 76th Street
                 Davenport, IA 52806

- -

ORDER BLANK

NAME _____

ADDRESS _____

CITY & STATE _____ ZIP _____

How many copies? _____ Amount enclosed _____
    Price per book $12.00
    Postage & handling 2.50
    Total $14.50
Please make checks payable to:
                 The Machine Shed
Mail orders to: Country Holiday Favorites
                 111 W. 76th Street
                 Davenport, IA 52806